MW01016232

Power in the Eye

THE UNIVERSITY OF CALGARY BOOKSTORE
2500 UNIVERSITY DRIVE NW.
CALGARY, ALBERTA T2N 1N4
403-220-5937   1-877-220-5 7
WWW.CALGARYBOOKSTORE.CA
GST #108102864

SALE   001 007 RC-1609997
CASHIER: 26   06/23/09 13:23

01 BYRNE / POWER IN THE EYE:
   101010 11199458   1 T   57.95

                      Subtotal   57.95
                      5% GST   2.90

      Items   1   Total   60.85

BANK DEBIT CARD   60.85
Acct Type: CHECKING
Acct: ****************7888
  Auth Cd: 203792
  Term ID: 66044257

               Change Due   0.00

        14 DAY RETURN POLICY
   MUST HAVE THIS ORIGINAL RECEIPT
     SHOP ONLINE 24 HRS A DAY
     WWW.CALGARYBOOKSTORE.CA

Refunds accepted within
14 days of purchase.
Must have original sales receipt.

Books must be in MINT condition.
Clothing products must not be
washed or worn and in original
condition with tags intact.

No refunds on sale items, film,
special orders, calculators, batteries,
medical, or personal care products.

The Bookstore retains the right
to refuse any refund.
Photo ID required at time of refund.

View our complete refund policy at:
www.calgarybookstore.ca

UNIVERSITY OF
CALGARY
BOOKSTORE

Power in the Eye

An Introduction to Contemporary Irish Film

Terry Byrne

The Scarecrow Press, Inc.
Lanham, Md., & London
1997

SCARECROW PRESS, INC.

Published in the United States of America
by Scarecrow Press, Inc.
4720 Boston Way
Lanham, Maryland 20706

4 Pleydell Gardens, Folkestone
Kent CT20 2DN, England

British Library Cataloguing in Publication Information Available

Library of Congress Cataloging-in-Publication Data

Byrne, Terry.
    Power in the eye : an introduction to contemporary Irish film /
Terry Byrne.
        p.   cm.
    Includes bibliographical references and index.
    ISBN 0-8108-3296-8 (cloth : alk. paper)
    1. Motion pictures—Ireland. I. Title.
PN1993.5.I85B97   1997
791.43'09417—dc21   97-5509

ISBN 0–8108–3296–8 (cloth : alk. paper)

CONTENTS

PREFACE

Ireland may be said to be an emergent nation; after centuries of domination by its neighbor, Britain, it fought its way to independence only to plunge into a self-imposed isolation for the next forty years. Thus it is that, in the last decade of the century, the country is experiencing a late reemergence into world consciousness.

This is both a process of address to the outside world and a means of self-definition. It is political, industrial, cultural, and creative: it finds expression in literature, music, drama, art, and cinema. In cultural and artistic terms, it is a time of great energy and excitement, especially for the young Irish who (though they may not be fully aware of it) are providing the driving force behind these changes.

Finding a voice is both exhilarating and frustrating. It is proving, as it ought, to be a contentious experience. Much of the subject matter has been fought over, and many minds have clashed repeatedly in the course of change. In a cultural context, this may be seen to be a good thing--anything so important should not come too easily, lest it be undervalued.

It is on this basis that one should interpret the new indigenous cinema of Ireland: as a means of national expression and as a tool for dialogue and address essential to the process of self-definition. By contrast, the United States, as landlord for the multinational film industry, may be the poorer, as the efforts made by American filmmakers to address their home audience may tend to be quashed by the monolithic Hollywood machine. With that in mind, we may learn much from the work of our Irish counterparts.

Under the auspices of the Film Institute of Ireland, various resources for filmmaking have been drawn together under one roof in the Irish Film Centre, Dublin. Many of the Irish colleges offer programs in film production, theory, and criticism. There are several film festivals around the country, with new ones appearing all the time (both North and South). Coupled with its large pool of young literate creative talent, Ireland seems poised for emergence into world consciousness in yet another arena.

ACKNOWLEDGMENTS

As a learning experience, the researching of this book was unique. I have found the subject to be far richer than I'd imagined, and have encountered many people whose generosity and encouragement have been both overwhelming and refreshing.

Without the interest and support of Sunniva O'Flynn and her colleagues at the Irish Film Archive, there would be no book. Their dedication to the collection and preservation of all kinds of material relating to Irish cinema seems to have no limits. I have made liberal use of the publications of Film Base (Centre for Film and Video), also housed in the new Irish Film Centre, and equally committed to the idea of an Irish cinema, on its own merit, as a worthy cause.

I've also been helped and encouraged by several members of the Irish filmmaking community, notably Joe Comerford, Kevin Rockett, Cathal Black, and Tommy McArdle. They have patiently answered my questions, put me in touch with ideas and resources, and provided material support in the form of production stills, documentation, and tickets to screenings. Thanks are also due to Terry George in New York, Pat Collins of *Film West* in Galway, John O'Regan of Gandon Editions, John Moore of Clingfilms, and Tom Murphy.

Finally, I would like to acknowledge the College of New Jersey for grant assistance, and Keith and Mary Hyland for their hospitality.

CHAPTER ONE
THE POWER OF THE IMAGE

James Joyce is synonymous with the modern view of Ireland: his uncompromising portrayal of the Irish people as he knew them, and the consequential banning of his most famous novel in his own country (and his lifelong expatriation) are typical of the relationship the country has had with many of its foremost artists in this century. It is fittingly ironic, then, that Joyce was one of the first entrepreneurs to open a cinema in Ireland (the Volta, in 1909).

Unquestionably, the relationship between those who would regulate the work of Ireland's filmmakers and those filmmakers themselves has been as contentious as the relationship between those forces of control and Ireland's writers. It is important to understand this relationship, since its impact has been direct and sometimes unsubtle, and has affected the whole of Irish society and culture in recent history.

The first film censorship law was enacted in 1923. This was amended in 1930, but not significantly, and the intended cultural and moral impact of film censorship has been continuously in operation from the outset. In the early days of self-rule, when the Free State had been established and the British government and military presence had been withdrawn, the Irish government adopted something of an isolationist policy: Gaelic was made the official first language of the country and made mandatory for anyone seeking civil service employment. (This policy may well have proved to be more harmful to the language than anything the British had done over the centuries to dissuade the Irish from speaking it.)

Though the Irish constitution is officially protective of religious
freedom, the de facto influence of the Catholic Church was, until
recently, so powerful that the government dared not stand against it.
As a consequence of these factors, the film censor came to be a
powerful individual whose task it was to excise anything from a film
that could be deemed to be subversive to the moral teachings of the
Church (or a challenge to its authority) or a politically incorrect
intrusion on the officially defined version of "Gaelic culture."
Needless to say, the net result was a great amount of cutting or
outright banning of popular films. In the words of Joe Comerford:

> There was a conscious level at which the whole idea of art was
> undermined in favor of religion.   In other words, Catholicism
> would take care of the emotional needs of the people and the
> State would run the administration. The State would, as all
> states do, set up a consciousness for the people about what they're
> living in.   So, in a sense, there was a degree to which film was
> used as propaganda.   A lot of that was done through American and
> British film: you discouraged indigenous work which could have
> dealt with core issues like civil war, the economy,
> emigration, ownership of property. That was all buried and
> what came in (and I don't mean this as a criticism specifically), just
> inadvertently, the people who came in--mainly Americans--weren't
> terribly aware of what they were coming into. They were simply
> being utilized to give a (certain) notion of Ireland (both for
> outside consumption and also very much for inside consumption)
> so that up until the 70s, virtually everything Irish cinema was
> producing was a version which was quite palatable for the status
> quo in Ireland. [1]

The vagaries of the censor's brief led to the unlikely banning or
cutting of such films as *Gone with the Wind* and Chaplin's *The Great
Dictator*. The former was reckoned to be an advocacy of immoral
behavior, and the latter was banned as propaganda, presumably
because Ireland's official position of neutrality during the Second
World War required a denial to the public at home that a war was
going on at all. (Hence the reference throughout to the war as "The

Emergency.") It is somewhat ironic also that citizens of the Irish Free State (later the Republic) could easily cross the border into Northern Ireland to see many of the films that were unavailable at home, since the censorship system in Britain was more interested in British political issues than in the guardianship of public morality. This is reminiscent of the situation which has long obtained in regard to television and abortion: Irish TV was strictly censored, though the Irish viewer has long been able to receive the British channels, and now gets all those and more on cable. This has been reckoned to be all right, since much of what was seen on British television tended to reinforce the presumption among the Irish of their own moral superiority. By the same logic, abortion has been unavailable to Irish women, although more than a few have gone abroad for an extended visit and had it done there. This too was acceptable, because it didn't happen on Irish soil.

The legacy of the nationalist movement was an official policy of isolationism and a very narrow (and Church-defined) view of the sort of behavior that was acceptable. The self-image of the Irish people, together with the view of them projected to the outside world, was defined by the government of Eamon de Valera according to an idyllic (and largely mythical) picture of a hardy and self-sufficient agrarian culture. This is not the quaint view propagated by Hollywood in such films as *The Quiet Man* or *Darby O'Gill and the Little People*, which furthered the brogue-speaking argumentative-but-lovable drunk rightly regarded with contempt by the guardians of culture in Ireland. The image they preferred was that of Robert Flaherty's *Man of Aran*, depicting the hard lives of Aran Island fisherfolk who seemed to spend all their time fishing, praying, and gathering seaweed. (One is left to wonder if they ever slept and where their children came from.) It was a matter of some contention at the time, when it was revealed that scenes in the film were staged and the people portraying the peasants were not quite the unsophisticated simple folk they were made out to be. The political significance of this imagery was very powerful in Ireland, where the country--having thrown off the foreign oppressors--was deep in the throes of reinventing itself. The government was determined to take control of this process, and so films and books in Ireland were made subject to the scrutiny of government censorship.

Film censorship was carried out by one person, and the scope was largely unrestricted. A film could be banned outright or ordered to be reedited or reshot before permission for public performance was given. The fundamental charge to the censor was one of protection of public morals, but the brief was sufficiently broad that films could also be banned or mutilated because they presented an unacceptable political viewpoint.

For a time in the mid-1980s Frank Hall was the film censor, and brought with him the promise of a greater degree of liberalism, largely because Hall was a respected humorist, writer, and television performer with a presumed sensitivity to the medium and the makers of films.

It has been the case that the advances made under Hall have been expanded upon under his successor Sheamus Smith, though it is unlikely that a system of industry self-regulation (such as that at work in Hollywood) will eventually replace the government-appointed censor. Certainly the flourishing home-based film industry seems to bring pressure to bear on the government to interfere less frequently and less invasively, since the perception is that the films being made in Ireland are helping to alleviate the unemployment situation. (More later on that subject.) It seems, at least, that the older and stricter politically correct image of the Irish presented to themselves is no longer foremost among the censor's priorities, since films like *The Commitments* and *My Left Foot* were given unfettered general release in Ireland and abroad while portraying the Irish in much less flattering ways than those considered acceptable by the arbiters of cultural nationalism in the old days under de Valera. It is a matter of no small importance that Joe Comerford's adventure epic *Reefer and The Model* was allowed to have a public showing. Apart from taking swipes at the nouveau ascendancy, this film portrays as one of its heroes a cross-dressing bank-robbing ex-IRA man in a sexual liaison with a soldier of the Republic in a public toilet. Certainly this is not the acceptable stereotype of the Soldiers of Destiny from popular Irish mythology, as we shall see.

The image of the Irish portrayed by other cultures has been equally rigid and stereotypical, but for other reasons and with other consequences. The strongest externally generated image of the Irish has probably been the one popularized in Britain, rooted in the comic caricature of the music-hall (a form of popular theater akin to vaudeville or burlesque in this country). A great many Irish have emigrated to Britain over the centuries, and the two cultures have had a close, if contentious, relationship for over a thousand years; nevertheless, the stereotype of the stage Irishman in British popular culture has not been kind, and is still pervasive. This is the image of the broadly accented bumbler often portrayed with the red nose and slurred speech of the chronic alcohol abuser. Such a recent product as *Fawlty Towers* (the John Cleese sitcom produced by the BBC and aired here on PBS) has trotted out this caricature in the form of a lazy carpenter who has killed so many brain cells with drink that he's unable to build a wall in the right place.

One of the requisites of conquest is the need to dehumanize the victim and thus alleviate any troublesome feelings of guilt. The portrayal of the Irish people as inherently flawed--shiftless, lazy, and often drunk--relieved the English of the need to treat them humanely and permitted the characterization of the conquest and plunder of Ireland as something of a noble gesture. Thus, the stage Irishman who became the staple of music-hall comedy served a deeper purpose by cementing in the popular imagination the idea that the Empire was a benevolent and Christian one, and in some way the expression of God's will. This image so pervaded English culture that some stage Irishmen were even portrayed by descendants of Irish immigrants, their surnames lending further credence to the myth. Having been so long established in English theater tradition, it was only natural that this stereotype carried over into film and television, where it lives today.

It is somewhat ironic that both the English and the nationalist

Irish were engaged in the same game, but with very different
objectives. The English caricatured the Irish in order to deny them
their cultural complexity and make it easier to dismiss their concerns.
The nationalist government in Ireland, on the other hand, was busily
creating a stereotype which would ennoble the Irish in their own eyes
and serve as a source of pride (and, more importantly, political
loyalty). In fact, the overwhelmingly important effect both distortions
had on the Irish people was to deny them a public expression of their
true character--weak and strong, gombeens[2] and great poets. On the
one hand, they were presented with a silly and degrading image, and
on the other, a mythical one which was not consistent with their
knowledge of themselves and was based upon a notion of Ireland's
relationship to the world which was largely unrealistic and ultimately
doomed to fail.

And then there was the American stereotype. In such films as
Darby O'Gill and the Little People or *The Quiet Man*, the biases
inherent in the American view of the Irish were exposed in equally
ludicrous caricatures. Drawn in some measure from the de Valeran
idyll, the American stereotype was usually of a country bumpkin with
a homespun-and-tweed wardrobe, blackthorn stick, and clay pipe. He
always spoke with a ridiculous brogue (the like of which never passed
the lips of any living Irishman), a fondness for whiskey, and a violent
temper. The net result was something of a cross between the other two
images, given a sort of rustic charm and mystique that appealed to
American tastes. (The success of *Far and Away* would indicate that
the market for this caricature is alive and well even today.)

The common thread here, of course, is the fact that each of these
stereotypical images was the result of an attempt to alter reality to suit
someone's specific agenda. As a result, they are all inaccurate in
varying degrees and (as do all such stereotypes) succeed only in
denying the subject people the true variety and complexity of their real
selves in the context of their actual society. In the case of the Irish,
this has been most unfortunate: Irish people come in a great many
variants (especially for a small country), and to simplify them thus is
to deny the depth and complexity of thought and creative talent

that Irish writers and artists have contributed to the culture of the larger society.

Many of the Irish have seen this, and it hasn't sat well with them. Hilton Edwards, the great theatrical director who gave the young Orson Welles his start, said this about *The Quiet Man*: " I cannot for the life of me see that it has any relation to the Ireland I or anyone else can have seen or known."[3]   This judgment may be applied to most of the films about Ireland produced for world distribution prior to *My Left Foot*.   With this film, the Irish were able to see themselves portrayed on the world stage in a light that was familiar to them, and the way was opened for further more realistic portrayals.   Jim Sheridan was by no means the first to show the Irish on film in a reasonably accurate manner, but he was among the first to attain a significant measure of world attention with a film which did so. Certainly a number of his contemporaries had shown a truer picture of Irish life to film audiences in the Irish and English markets--notably Neil Jordan, Pat Murphy, Cathal Black, and Joe Comerford. *My Left Foot,* however, was a milestone: from the raucous applause it received at the New York Film Festival to the Academy Awards, the combination of a strong personal/emotional story and a gritty-but-enchanting portrait of Dublin life in the 1950s opened up to many people a subtly revisionist message quietly debunking some of the stereotypical myths about Irish character.   Sheridan and Noel Pearson (the film's producer) had set about making a film about their city which was true to their experience of it but also defined a new world market for films which were *about* Ireland rather than merely *set* there.

If you suppose from this that the world's perception of the nature of the Irish is characterized by ignorance, you are not far from the truth. For a variety of reasons, the Irish had for many years not found a voice in the world. This may be, in part, because theirs is a predominantly verbal culture in a world in which the importance of the word has been devalued, or it may be because of the years of isolationism and the suppression of free expression. Nonetheless, the world view of the Irish has closely adhered to the stereotype of the sloppy drunk and natural combatant, and nowhere more so than in the United States.

In a climate in which the preferred media of expression and information are television and film, a people who still gravitate toward the written word and the theater for their creative vehicles have had difficulty getting that word out to the larger audience. When the Americans and British looked at television news stories depicting Ireland, they saw scenes of violence from Northern Ireland and concluded that there was shooting and bombing going on in the Republic as well. (I recently received in the mail a brochure offering video travelogues for sale that referred to Belfast and Dublin as the two great cities of Northern Ireland!)[4] Most of the English-speaking world has become rather simplistically-minded, demanding quick solutions and information delivered in superficial overviews. We garner our knowledge of the world from half-hour television news programs (an hour if we consider ourselves intellectuals) whose bias is toward topics which make "good pictures" and those with violent or sensational content.

In such a context, a society whose culture is distinguished by the complexity and subtlety of its verbal expression is inherently handicapped. Thus it is that the American view of Ireland is still reliant upon the work of Joyce, Synge and O'Casey: back when our culture was also a verbal one, they were categorized as great writers and their work entered into our lists of classics. Regrettably, the work of many more recent authors and dramatists has gone substantially unrecognized because their skills with language were not valued in the larger world and they were not brash or violent enough to make themselves heard.

This is not to say that there has not been a proliferation of new work from Ireland. There has been quite a number of writers and dramatists producing new and exciting work--for the home audience. Partly because of the need to take control themselves of the process of cultural definition, and partly because Ireland, as an emergent nation, finds itself in an odd position among English-speaking countries, much of the best talent in Ireland has found itself speaking to its own country rather than representing Irish ideas to the outside world. In this effort, the writers and artists to emerge recently have found an eloquence and wit equal to that of their more famous predecessors.

This is the world's loss. The containment of the writing of Tom Murphy, Dermot Bolger, and others to the Irish audience has deprived the rest of the world of some of the finest wordsmithing and dramatic skill to have come from Ireland. This is doubly frustrating, because these are the works of a more sophisticated and worldly Ireland than that which existed in the past, and little of this work is so obscure or written in such thick dialect as to be incomprehensible to someone outside the Irish experience. All the universal themes are at work in these pieces, and the issues and emotions dealt with accessible to people everywhere. Nonetheless, only a few of Murphy's plays have been produced professionally outside Ireland, and the same is true of many of his contemporaries.

There is, however, a positive side, evidenced by the fact that things have begun to turn around. Partly due to an increased Irish presence in popular music and partly due to the international success of several recent films, the word has begun to spread that Ireland harbors a number of very talented artists whose strange position as members of the English-speaking community, though not fully assimilated into its mass culture, gives them a unique perspective and a voice worth hearing. It is thus a phenomenon of no small importance when several pivotal individuals find the tools and resources to present their work on the world stage and give the rest of us the opportunity to see things through their eyes. This situation has been a long time coming, and a number of people and institutions have been instrumental in the shaping of the conditions under which it has come about. This book is about those new visions which are being expressed on film and the forces which have been important in their formation.

A Note on Context

There are difficulties to be faced by anyone who wishes to pursue an interest in Irish filmmaking. Chief among these is the fact that much indigenous film product is unavailable outside Ireland.

Regrettably, much of it is unavailable there too. An extreme example of this problem is Tommy McArdle's film, *The Kinkisha*. The copy which I was able to view in the Irish Film Archive during the researching of this book may well be the only extant print. One might expect this where the film is, say, a very old one from the 1920s or 30s; this film, however, is less than twenty years old. This is a problem in a mass-market medium: if a film gets general distribution, there are many copies struck; if not, there may be only a handful. Understandably, the archivists in Dublin are reluctant to lend their prints of such films, and the cost of striking additional prints may not be financially justified, making some virtually inaccessible. Remarkably, some are available on vidoetape (particularly those which were coproduced with European television companies). These video prints, however, are produced on the PAL format and will not play back on equipment in the NTSC format, such as is used in North and South America. I recommend the purchase of a multi-format VCR for this purpose.

Filmmaking is an art. One film may be more or less commercially oriented than another, but the making of the film itself is largely a subjective process. Commenting about film content is also a subjective process; the same film will frequently say different things to different people. I would, therefore, urge anyone with a serious interest to do her best to view these films firsthand and reach her own conclusions about them. (I will list resources at the end of the book to help with this.)

Additionally, this book--like computer software--will necessarily be out of date almost as soon as it is published. This subject is an ongoing one (mushrooming, in fact) and many new films are in production as this goes to press. Still, I hope to give a bit of background information to the newcomer about the people, process, and history of recent film production in Ireland to help him put it into perspective. Mostly, though, I hope to challenge some preconceptions and aid the reader in approaching Irish films with an open mind.

Finally, the book is necessarily less than comprehensive. I have refrained from comment about films I have not seen; the inclusion of second hand commentary would not have been particularly helpful. Thus, there is a great deal of material that is not touched upon here. I can only recommend that the reader pursue it himself, and am willing to warrant that it will be a most rewarding pursuit. There are many short films, documentaries, and animated pieces which have not been included (due to time and travel constraints) and are surely worth seeking out.

Notes

1. Author's interview with Joe Comerford, 26 June 1994.
2. In Irish Gaelic, a "gombeen" is a clever swindler or usurer, often disguised beneath the appearance of a simple country person.
3. Quoted in Brian McIlroy, *Irish Cinema* (Dublin: Anna Livia Press, 1988): 41.
4. The two urban centers of Northern Ireland are Belfast and Derry City (or Londonderry). All the other large Irish cities are in the Republic.

CHAPTER TWO
NATIONALIZING THE INDUSTRY

Ardmore: The National Film Studios of Ireland (NFSI)

Ten miles south of Dublin, located along a sandy beach, is the old resort town of Bray, in County Wicklow. It's a classic Victorian relic of a type found all over Ireland and England: rows of old guesthouses, restaurants, and beachfront amusements connected to the nearest city by a rail line and dependent on weekend and holiday trade for its survival. It is important to remember this when considering the Irish government's decision to locate the National Film Studios of Ireland there.

In the spring of 1958, shooting began on *Home Is The Hero,* an adaptation of a stage play by Walter Macken which was transported to the film studios from the Abbey Theatre in Dublin. This was the first feature shot in the NFSI, which is locally known simply as "Ardmore," the name of the estate on which it was built. When the government of Ireland decided to throw off the mantle of isolationist politics and enter the world economy, it was done without much reserve, and perhaps with a bit too much naivete: there are still empty factory buildings here and there standing as testimony to the fickleness of some multinational (read American and Japanese) corporations who abandoned them when the tax deferments ran out. In this regard, Ardmore was no exception, and the studios were built on a grand scale, well equipped, and opened with a lot of hoopla and projections of profitability which have never come true.

Ardmore Studios were built to attract foreign capital and provide employment for Irish craftspeople in a highly paid industry. Newspaper articles from that time indicate that the important considerations were the size of the sound stages and the inclusion of a water tank for shooting underwater scenes. In addition to the five stages, there were carpentry, prop, and costume shops, dressing rooms, catering facilities, and an onsite nightclub. The entire facility was conceived as a self-contained unit (even growing vegetables and grazing farm animals), isolated from the communities surrounding it. In fact, what was built was something of a cross between a film studio and a resort--and the implications of that fact are important. The following quote is from the *Irish Press* of 29 January 1958:

> . . . it is hoped that Ardmore Studios will be entirely self-contained--even to providing its own meat, vegetables, and dairy-produce for the canteen and the plush-lined 'Stars' dining-club which will be situated in the mansion. As for costumes, scenery, furniture and furnishings for the sets, they will be made on the premises. A vast workshop 280 ft. long by 60 ft. wide, will house shops for painters, plasterers, and carpenters, a wood- working mill, 'property' stores and a complete service workshop. It is stressed that Ardmore Studios is primarily an Irish industry, financed with Irish capital, and its proud intention is to employ Irish technicians and Irish labour wherever humanly possible. But film-making is so highly skilled in almost every one of its many branches, needing years of specialized training, that it will obviously be quite a while before there will be anything like a 100 per cent Irish staff at Ardmore. (To expedite this, a training-school for Irish would-be technicians is to be established.)

Note the thrust of the article: Ardmore was to be established to attract foreign capital into the country for the purpose of employing *"Irish labour."* From the outset, the context in which the National Film Studios has been operated was an industrial one. Casting around for various industries that the government might seek to attract in order to accelerate the industrialization of the Irish economy, they lit upon film production as a promising candidate. This point of view has predominated in successive Irish governments, and its persistence has fueled much of the controversy between those governments and some of the members of the indigenous filmmaking community.

On its face, this controversy revolves around a single issue: would the National Film Studios be used to make films for the Irish audience, or would they become simply a means of providing access to Ireland as a scenic backdrop for films which are committed neither to addressing the Irish nor even portraying them in a realistic light? Nearly forty years on, it is still a source of contentiousness. At the showing of *Anne Devlin* in New York in June of 1994, Pat Murphy (the film's director) expressed to me her dismay that the farm country in the west of Ireland was being used as a picturesque backdrop for Hollywood epics such as *Far and Away* without addressing the human toll and the political and economic reasons behind the abandonment of those farms, which are now so picturesque because no one lives there any longer. There is a very tangible and probably quite justified sense

1. The National Film Studios at Ardmore, County Wicklow. (Courtesy of the Irish Film Archive)

among the community of indigenous filmmakers that resources allocated to the promotion of film production have gone into these foreign projects at the expense of indigenous production. Over the years, the answer has been made quite clear: the studios at Ardmore are there for rental to the highest bidder, strictly as a business venture made by the government to attract foreign investment.

This is not to say that the existence of the studios has never benefited any indigenous filmmaking, but rather that the facilities have been pitched to clients outside the country, and fees and services priced at a rate typically payable only by British and American corporate filmmakers. Especially since Ireland joined the European Community, the prices charged for goods and services have not been especially competitive, and Ardmore has occasionally failed to attract investment from American backers when labor was found to be cheaper even in California. The combined effects of the strength of the Irish pound ("punt" is the Gaelic word) on the world market and the failure to build a core of native users has meant that the film studios have had a roller-coaster history of closure, bankruptcy, receivership, and State bailouts--a long way from the projections of profitability being made at the opening in 1958.

It is significant that the last item touted in the newspaper article quoted above was the establishment of a "training-school" for Irish film technicians, a thing that never happened. Throughout the history of the NFSI, few of the technicians above the grades of craftspeople (in other words, carpenters, electricians, grips, and other support trades) were Irish. Most of the directors, production designers, directors of photography, and the other creative and senior management personnel came from the British industry. This is only natural, given the situation: if a film is conceived in Britain and backed with British money, the senior creatives and other managerial staff are going to be hired from within the producers' own market, Britain, just as are the featured actors. In the same way that one gets Tom Cruise attempting to portray an Irishman in *Far and Away,* a film made in Ireland, one also finds the more important creative and technical jobs being meted out to British and American personnel in the sort of high-risk big-budget feature film which Ardmore was designed to accommodate.

That said, the National Film Studios have managed to survive in spite of being handicapped by having no particular brief under which to operate, apart from that of making money. As observers in Ireland have noted, the strange thing about Ardmore was its lack of an operating identity: it was strictly a "four wall" facility whose use for any given period of time was determined by the needs of a preexisting outside production company whose only goals were short-term ones (as is true of most film production companies). Some theaters on Broadway or in London's West End are run in similar fashion, but with two distinct differences: they maintain virtually no permanent staff apart from the rental office, and they play an active role in the profit-taking (i.e., box office). As originally structured, Ardmore missed the mark on both these points, attempting to provide permanent employment for a fairly sizable staff and taking no role in the distribution of films produced there. It was a very naive and ill-informed undertaking, and a losing proposition from its inception, and yet successive Irish governments have bailed it out over and over again.

In 1978, when the management of Ardmore were begging the government for a grant of 150,000 punts, the studios were paying roughly one-third of their outgoings to debt service on previous loans. At that time, the studios' carpentry shops were taking on architectural work and the open land surrounding the soundstages was being rented to car importers as a storage area prior to distribution to various dealerships. Sometimes the soundstages were rented to commercial clients for use in product launches and other live events of that kind, but the essential message of all this is simple and clear: as a commercial film studio operation, the National Film Studios were a dismal failure.

John Boorman was brought in as studio chairman in the hope

that his reputation as a film director would lend the place credibility and make it attractive.   Nonetheless, in 1982, a year after he had finished *Excalibur*, Boorman was announcing his resignation. At that time, the studios were losing about 700,000 punts every year and carrying a debt of nearly 2 million.   In March of that year, the government announced its intention to close the studios, a decision made by the Minister for Industry, Albert Reynolds (who was later to become prime minister).   Reynolds was quoted as saying that the studios were "not essential to an Irish film industry"[1] and a plan was mooted to sell off the soundstages to a film company and much of the adjoining land to developers.

Surprisingly, a buyer was found very quickly.   Vincent Donohoe, a Florida-based businessman with strong Irish connections, announced plans to make Ardmore into a video production facility.   This was greeted with some relief by the Irish government which was anxious to get the white elephant off its hands, but Donohoe failed to get sufficient backing and the deal evaporated.

Two more years elapsed, and a new industry minister (and Reynolds' successor as prime minister), John Bruton, announced the sale of the studios to Pakistani film producer Mahmud Sipra.   Sipra paid a million punts for the studios, but was unable to finance necessary repairs to make the place operational, and soon they were once again in receivership.

Eventually, the National Film Studios were acquired by a consortium led by MTM in conjunction with Morgan O'Sullivan's company, Tara Productions.   Again, the target market was to be television, with MTM using Ardmore as its European base of production operations. Since then, the studios have operated as a sort of street market for film production, with a number of independent facility suppliers leasing space from which to provide support services. They have seen a rise in television-commercial production (on film) together with a certain amount of feature production, a combination that has made the facility relatively lucrative, at least by comparison with its previous record. Whether this has anything to do with the operation and marketing of Ardmore or just a reflection of a trend in the industry, and driven by influences outside the studios themselves, the result is that there is now a reasonable market for the services the studios provide.

It is, indeed, a long way from the inflated aspirations of 1958 and resembles very little the kind of mini-Hollywood-cum-resort that the government of that time imagined it would be, but it is good that, as the demand for such a studio has materialized, the studios are there to be made useful. It is ironic, especially, that the Irish people working there were not trained in the Studios themselves (since the training facility as originally proposed never came into being), but are largely the product of the independent filmmaking community and learned their crafts in art college, Radio Telefis Eireann[2], or "on the ground" (i.e., by teaching themselves). As a model for governmental involvement in the film "industry" Ardmore stands as an example of the halfway effort and underlying mistrust which has characterized successive Irish governments' other dealings with the film community.

The Film Board: Bord Scannan Na hEireann (BSE)

After years of criticism from the indigenous film community (small though that may have been), an effort was made in the early eighties to address film in a context other than the industrial. The thinking behind Ardmore's establishment had been of the "if we build it, they will come" sort, and the reluctance of the government to invest in the front-end part of the process belied its attitude toward the making of films--simply as a device to attract foreign capital to Irish coffers.

The BSE's second chairman, Muiris Mac Conghail, stated succinctly the embarrassing fact about the Ardmore experience:

> The history of the industry in Ireland has been one of trying to make
> Irish films with other people's money. The result cannot be
> surprising--we have made other people's films for other
> people.[3]

He was, as it happens, merely stating the view held (and publicly
made) by a number of filmmakers in Ireland at the time. In 1977/78, a
group of film people (led by Tiernan MacBride, Michael Algar, Bob
Quinn, and others) had formed the Association of Irish Film Makers
(AIFM), which grew out of contact with and encouragement from a
similar affiliation in Britain, the Association of Independent
Producers.

As a result of lobbying activity, 1979 saw the introduction by Des
O'Malley (then Minister for Industry) of the Film Board Bill to the
Dail[4]. (Note, yet again, that the matter of film production is being
broadly categorized by government under the "industry" heading.)
Due partly to lack of interest on the part of the government, the AIFM
managed to propose and effect a number of significant amendments to
the bill. Although these did not go quite as far as the AIFM would
have liked, it was a matter of some importance that the bill as enacted
included provision for craft training, the establishment of a film
archive, and a "hands-off" policy regarding the content of works
funded by the Board. So, while the film censor continued to dictate
the content of feature films certified for public presentation, the
indigenous filmmaking community had begun steps toward the
reduction of censorship, at least as far as Irish-originated projects were
concerned.

From the outset, however, the BSE had been only a little more
than a token gesture. In its first incarnation (it ceased operations for a
number of years) from 1981-1987, the average fund available for
investment in new projects was a half-million punts a year. In
addition, the premise under which it was established was that the
money disbursed was really only a loan, and the filmmaker recipients
were liable for the repayment of it. Virtually none of the money
invested was ever paid back. This was the reason given for the

closure of BSE's operations in 1987. Its legacy, though, was not to
have had a great impact upon the sort of low-end grassroots
indigenous production it was presumably meant to encourage. By the
end of its first phase, the board had drifted back toward the "film as
industry" brief, and the plan offered in place of the defunct BSE was a
system of tax breaks for investors in film projects under the Finance
Act of 1987 and a subsequent Business Expansion Scheme.[5] As with
Ardmore, this plan too came to be seen as a means of attracting
foreign capital.

It was not until 1993 that change was to come, and it was
dramatic change. In March of that year, the BSE was resurrected.
Not only was it resurrected; this time it was placed under the aegis of a
new department and a new minister for Arts, Culture, and the
Gaeltacht[6] and given a substantially larger budget than in its previous
life. This minister was Michael D. Higgins, and his nominee for the
chairmanship of the Board was Lelia Doolan, a longtime spokesperson
for the indigenous film and theater communities and a former Radio
Telefis Eireann producer. This, together with the establishment of the
Irish Film Centre in Dame Street (bringing together the film archives,
cinemas, and the Film Base support center) finally showed tangible
evidence of an Irish government willing to take its own film
community seriously.

Arguably, this was belated and perhaps less than convincing
evidence of any unusual enlightenment. It should be noted in that
context that this action came only on the heels of Jim Sheridan's
Oscar-winning work in *My Left Foot,* and the critical successes of Neil
Jordan and others. It is probable that the international acclaim
garnered by certain Irish film talent and the ensuing financial
successes had some effect in swaying the collective political mind
toward the support of the native film community. It was only after
several notable commercially successful projects and some
exhaustively documented reports on the state of filmmaking in Ireland
that the political community decided that this horse was safe enough

to be backed. It may be worth noting that the taoiseach (prime minister) under whose aegis the new support for filmmaking came was none other than Albert Reynolds, who had closed Ardmore in 1982 when he was minister for industry.

During the hiatus between Film Boards, the only noncommercial sources of funding for independent filmmakers were the Arts Council (An Comhairle Ealaion) and RTE. By comparison with the Film Board, such grants as were available from these sources were small, and mostly targeted script development rather than production costs.

The involvement of RTE in the film community will be dealt with in the next chapter, and that took many forms, but the Arts Council's support for film in the 1987-92 period (during the BSE hiatus) was approximately a half-million punts.

As a means of stimulating the industry, the original Film Board was not particularly successful. It was not generously funded, being able to dole out only seed money in the hopes of generating thereby the larger amounts required for feature production, and none of its beneficiary films achieved any sort of international commercial success. Films like *My Left Foot, The Commitments,* and *In the Name of the Father* were developed with money from British and American investors, largely independently from the agencies of the Irish government.

As a stimulus for indigenous production, however, the Board did have an impact, and a number of films which were significant to the home audience were made possible through its financial assistance. Notable among these were Bob Quinn's *Atlantean,* Cathal Black's *Our Boys* and *Pigs,* and Pat Murphy's *Anne Devlin.* These "loans" ranged in amount from 5,000 to 30,000 punts and, as noted before, were rarely repaid.

What is startling, but also quite significant, is the choice of Rod Stoneman for CEO of the new Film Board. Stoneman is British. He made his mark, however, as commissioning editor for Channel Four in Britain (the newest television channel, BBC 1, BBC 2, and ITV being the others) directed at the minority audiences. We will refer to Channel Four in the next chapter, but it should be noted here that one of the most important things it has done was the commissioning of film drama from independents all over the British Isles. Both in terms of payment for the practice of their craft and in terms of exposure to a wider audience, the impact of Channel Four has been a powerful one. Many of the films produced by indigenous Irish talent in recent years have been commissioned, at least in part, by Channel Four.

At the annual general meeting of Film Base in March 1994, Stoneman stunned the audience by announcing, "There is no such thing as an Irish film industry, nor is there ever likely to be one."[7] He then proceeded to define his terms, whereupon it became clear that he regards only Los Angeles and Bombay as having sufficient indigenous audience to support a film industry. In other words, he has clearly indicated that the film community in Ireland should no longer be regarded strictly as an industrial venture, because the limited home market virtually guarantees commercial failure. All this would seem to bode well for those filmmakers: the establishment of the new Film Board under the banner of "Arts" as opposed to "Industry" and the appointment of a director whose vision of that endeavor is a noncommercial one made the future seem just a bit rosier.

That said, it should also be noted that the funds provided by the new Film Board are still regarded as loans, to be repaid from any profits the films might make. After the first year of operation, the tendency has also been toward commercially viable films. *Korea,* for instance--a new film with Irish themes and using Irish talent--was largely funded outside the country although some support was forthcoming from the Film Board after the project was under way. By contrast, *Circle Of Friends,* which was largely a foreign production, received substantial investment from the Film Board. The attraction of commercialism is still strong. Cathal Black, director of *Korea,* is still slightly hopeful that the needs of both sorts of films can be met:

It takes time and energy. It takes some money, obviously,

but more than that it takes the will.   It's difficult; you don't
see quick results.   You need to sit down and say, "We're
going to nourish this--it's going to take time."[8]

Notes

1. Cian O hEigeartaigh, "Boorman Quits as Reynolds Shuts
Ardmore," *Sunday Tribune,* 4 April 1982.

2. Radio Telefis Eireann is the Irish television company.

3. David Orr, "An Injection to Ease Film's Demise," *Irish Times,*
27 May 1982, 7.

4. The Dail is the parliament of the Republic of Ireland.

5. Kevin Rockett, "Culture, Industry, and Irish Cinema," in
Border Crossing: Film in Ireland, Britain, and Europe, John Hill,
Martin McLoone, and Paul Hainsworth, eds.   (Belfast/London:
Institute for Irish Studies/British Film Institute, 1994), 126-139.

6. The gaeltacht is the term (in both Gaelic and English) for
those areas in Ireland in which Irish Gaelic is still the first language.

7. Hugh Linehan, "Not the Irish Film Industry," *Film Ireland*
issue 40 (April/May 1994): 13-14.

8. Author's interview, 27 July 1995.

CHAPTER THREE
SMALL-SCREEN FILMS

If, as Rod Stoneman would have us believe, there is no hope of developing a true film industry in Ireland, then funding for film production by indigenous directors must necessarily come from outside sources. The term "outside" may be taken to mean foreign capital, or it may be taken to mean Irish capital from sources outside the film community. Or, indeed, it may be both.

Certainly much of the funding for feature production, regardless of the "Irishness" of the creative talent involved, has come from abroad. It is safe to say that few, if any, of the more recent ventures could have been funded entirely from domestic sources. Aside from the more obvious films featuring foreign talent in front of the lens or in the director's chair, the smaller-budget feature-length projects developed in and for the Irish market have also been largely financed from abroad. Typically, the production money comes from Britain, the United States, and Europe. (Europeans seem to like Irish subjects, and the populations of immigrant Irish and people of Irish descent in the United States and Britain virtually guarantee the audience there.) Foreign interest and investment notwithstanding, the typical annual production schedule (even in these times of increased activity) has averaged less than ten such projects in recent years. In 1993, for example, eight features were completed with budgets ranging from a million pounds to 9.2 million, with a total of only 34 million for the year's production. Compared with Los Angeles feature production, these are small projects indeed and the budget figures would seem to support Stoneman's contention.

As long as the feature-film industry remains geographically centralized as it is now, there is little hope that anything like a large-scale infusion of business will fall Ireland's way. On the other hand, the television industry seems to be in the process of decentralizing in many countries, and may show some prospects for evolving into a global cottage industry of a high-tech sort. As production of television and film-for-television in North America drifts away from Los Angeles to places like Vancouver, Florida, New York, and even Baltimore, so production in Britain has begun to move out of London. Although the British film industry (if we propose that it once had one) was not especially long-lived, it left behind several compact but productive facilities in and around London at places like Ealing, Elstree, and Shepperton. These have been utilized for television productions, originated both on tape and film, for some years. However, under pressure from government, production in the BBC and ITV networks has been spread more evenly around the country, moving to Pebble Mill, Manchester, Bristol, and elsewhere. The monolithic BBC studios compound in Shepherd's Bush (London) has seen severe staff reductions over the past few years as the production operation was decentralized throughout the BBC system.

The reason for this is the essentially noncommercial nature of all broadcasting in Britain. The BBC is supported entirely by license fees--a sort of annual tax applied to all owners of television receivers--and the independent networks, while allowed advertising, are strictly restricted as to how much and how often. The result has been a much greater sense of television as a public service rather than a commercial venture, and the governing bodies have seen to it that television production companies in Britain have been more closely accountable to their audiences than have the television networks in the United States. As a response to complaints that television in Britain was too much concentrated in the southeast (both geographically and culturally) the BBC and ITV both strove to establish more substantial production facilities in provincial locales. Coupled with this was the drive to do more regionally targeted production, and to make use of those locations with more film and film-style shooting. Thus we have seen more dramatic serials and single "feature" productions placed in Yorkshire or Wales or Scotland, and fewer multi-camera productions originating from London studios.

All this, however, was not enough. In addition to a trend toward decentralization of the existing channels, there was the establishment of Channel Four (S4C in Wales) to address the minority populations in Britain. Of course one of the largest minority populations in Britain is Irish--especially so if one expands the term to include the refugees from Northern Ireland (technically already citizens of Britain who fled to the mainland to escape the "Troubles." Channel Four has devoted a substantial amount of funding and airtime to Irish dramas, and Rod Stoneman was one of those who orchestrated that, hence his rather natural accession to the leadership of Bord Scannan na hEireann. These projects have included a mix of shorts, feature-length, commercial, and highly noncommercial ventures. Many have been of high quality and have had an impact upon those in Ireland who saw them. (Remember that approximately two-thirds of the population of Ireland can receive British television off-air, and a sizable number in addition to that get it via cable.) Thus it is that British viewers, by means of their support for British-produced television, have provided funding for independent Irish filmmakers speaking to an Irish audience (especially if we include in that the Irish diaspora in Britain).

Although Channel Four has been a significant source of funding for Irish film projects, the other British channels, such as the BBC (often via its Northern Ireland entity) and ITV have also been investors in them. Although the British channels have sometimes lost money on their Irish productions, they have continued to invest in them. Presumably, this has been considered a part of the public-service brief included in their charge; whatever the reason, the results have been quite impressive. Some of the better productions dealing with Irish subjects in recent years have been partly funded by British television: these include *Lamb, December Bride, High Boot Benny, Reefer and the Model, Eat the Peach, The Miracle, The Ballroom of Romance,* and *Angel.* They have also included some of the commercial successes, such as *My Left Foot, The Snapper,* and *The Crying Game.*

Notably absent from the list of funding sources in the same period--to the chagrin of Irish filmmakers--has been Radio Telefis Eireann, the Irish network. While the late seventies and early eighties saw some substantial undertakings by RTE, notably *Strumpet City* and *The Year of the French,* a cap on network revenues imposed by the government in the mid eighties caused a severe cutback in home-produced programming. This was felt in a reduction (almost to nothing) of RTE-produced drama, with the exception of its two long-running soap operas, *Glenroe* and *Fair City,* both of which are produced predominantly on videotape and neither of which can be considered dramas in the sense in which we use it in this discussion. As soaps, they have also been relegated to the sort of themes which revolve around domestic strife rather than confronting any of the more politically sensitive issues of social change that stand-alone film drama pieces presumably would.

The Television Films of Kieran Hickey

Casting back to the early 1980's (prior to the cutbacks), a number of films by Kieran Hickey were supported in part by RTE pre-sale investments, and these films (notably *Criminal Conversation* and *Exposure*) dealt with somewhat difficult topics and unembellished portrayals of Irish culture. Still, though RTE was an investor in Cathal Black's *Our Boys,* it was not broadcast by them until ten years later, perhaps indicating a reluctance on the part of the semi-state network to wade into waters which were too politically sensitive. Since *The Year of the French,* then, the Irish television network has been notable in the context of Irish film largely by its absence.

Recent developments, however, have brightened the prospects on that front as well. The government has lifted the revenue cap, and charged RTE with the funding and production of indigenous work, and the amounts of money involved are respectable ones. The sum available to commission new work in 1994 was 5 million punts, and the government has directed that this be increased to 12 million by the end of the century[1].

In the 1970s and 1980s, RTE had been both a source of revenue for Irish filmmaking and a source of trained talent. Tommy McArdle, Bob Quinn, Cathal Black, Joe Comerford, and Pat O'Connor all worked in RTE either prior to pursuing careers in independent film production or simultaneously with them. The television network once had a large and active film department, and many Irish film technicians learned their craft there. It has since been decommissioned, and the last remnant--the film processing lab--is in need of extensive repair and will likely be scrapped.

Much of the film work commissioned by RTE has been documentary. The long-running series *Radharc* ("vision" in English) was entirely produced by the Radharc Production Company (Peter Kelly and Joseph Dunn), which now boasts a catalog of over 350 pieces and is still going strong.

Also significant was the *Hands* series produced by David Shaw-Smith for RTE, and numerous scenic, historical, and nature films shot by Gerrit Van Gelderen and Eamon De Buitlear. These and other documentary and historical filmmakers have consistently worked to a very high technical and aesthetic standard and performed a significant service to the Irish in recording aspects of their culture which are now being or already have been left behind as the nation takes on more of the mainstream Euro-American culture.

That said, the work of Kieran Hickey stands apart as film-for-television which attempted, in the context of dramatic work, to address some aspects of Irish culture that may have been a little more contentious and emotive. The first of these was *Exposure,* which is set in the west of Ireland and revolves around three government surveyors who meet a French woman (a photographer, hence the title) and all compete for her attention. Two of the men are older and married, though neither of these facts seems to inhibit either of them in the pursuit of the photographer. Predictably, the younger single man finally wins her attention and goes off with her, leaving the older two alone in the hotel with the nosy old landlady (who seems to get her entertainment and titillation by listening in on all the guests' telephone calls). After a protracted drinking binge, punctuated by a lot of self-pitying whining, the older men sneak into the French woman's room and rifle through her underwear in a somewhat ritualistic perverse dance--in the middle of which they are interrupted by the couple's return. The morning after, however, is the critical part: the younger man, having done virtually nothing to defend or console the shaken and crying woman, rejoins his partners and they carry on much as they had before.

There are two significant factors about the woman apart from her gender: she is foreign and she is a photographer. The "exposure" referred to is revelation of the difficulty Irish men seem to have had in dealing with women, and the way in which women were relegated to a secondary role in much of Irish society. (We will see this theme again in *The Ballroom of Romance.*) These men are at ease only with themselves; they do not confide in their wives or seem to miss them much, and appear to regard the foreign woman as something of a prize, a spur to competition rather than a person. The younger man seems not to fit this mold entirely, and that may be the source of his appeal to the photographer, although he ultimately capitulates and rejoins the camaraderie, as it were. As a lone woman, a woman with a profession, and a foreigner, the photographer is both mysterious and desirable. More than that, as someone from outside Irish society and Irish mores, she is also fair game. Hickey is showing to his audience a side of Irish male culture that is essentially hypocritical: in much the same way that abortion is all right if it happens on British soil, so is adultery if it happens with a foreigner. With the device of the photographer and the ironic metaphor embodied in the title, he attempts to objectify the Irish male to himself. It's rather an ugly picture of fear, alienation, and repressed hostility stifled by drinking, underscored by a bleak documentary style of shooting at the beginning that becomes more oblique and much darker by the end.

Hickey followed this two years later (1980) with *Criminal Conversation*. Once again, the subject was sexual mores, but this time the piece was structured more carefully and the treatment was razor sharp. Where *Exposure* was set against the backdrop of the scenic rural west, *Criminal Conversation* (a legal term for adultery) is placed in the more urbane middle-class suburbs of Dublin. The players are members of the new business class, and (as before) none of them is particularly likable. The action follows a day in the life of Frank Murray, a corporate executive who is discovered making sexual advances on a secretary at the office Christmas party. In the middle of this exploit, his wife (Margaret) calls to remind him that they have a dinner party to attend. Annoyed, he goes home and flirts with the baby-sitter in front of his wife before the couple departs to the dinner, at the house of another married couple with whom they are friends. The dinner party soon deteriorates into squabbling similar to that of *Who's Afraid of Virginia Woolf?* and it transpires that Frank's wife and his friend Charlie (at whose house they are) have been having an affair. The couples get more intoxicated and the fighting becomes more bitter, in the midst of which Hickey takes us back several times to the baby-sitter, who is now entertaining her boyfriend at Frank and Margaret's house. Later, having left the dinner party, Frank crashes into the baby-sitter's party and sends the boyfriend away. Margaret then arrives with Charlie and discovers Frank apparently in a state of compromise with the baby-sitter. In the midst of the collapsing facades, Charlie utters the vague hope that they can all still be friends. Finally, Margaret goes to the bathroom, removes her wedding rings, and goes up to the bedroom where she collapses against the wall and stands, trancelike, switching the lights on and off. We then cut to an exterior shot of the bedroom window, flashing like a distress signal in the dark city.

This is very potent material. Hickey has addressed in this film the despair felt by those who have achieved material success at the expense of their emotional stability. The wisdom of Ireland's wholehearted embrace of capitalism in recent years and the unbridled greed that has become a part of business life in the pursuit of economic success is called into question here. The newly wealthy, who populate many of the suburbs of Ireland's cities, are shown to be morally and ethically bankrupt, condemned to lives of bickering marriage and loveless adulterous sex. Like his previous film, this one has a detached documentary tenor--perhaps even more detached--and the feel of an exercise in clinical observation. The parallel lines of action between the fighting couples and the baby-sitter and her boyfriend invite us to question whether the children of the new capitalists are doomed to suffer the same fate as their elders. There is no real note of relief; the possibility is left open that the young people may have some stronger sense of love or commitment, but it is only a possibility placed before us without any inflection to indicate what will become of them. In the same way that he used the bleak loneliness of the west to underscore the essential inhumanity of the protagonists in *Exposure*, Hickey has used the dysfunctional marriages of 1980s Dublin yuppies to illustrate the loneliness and desperation visited upon those whose relentless pursuit of greater material wealth has left them with empty lives.

In both these films, Kieran Hickey has grappled with the conflict engendered by Ireland's emergent status. The emergence from the mythical idyll of de Valera and the isolationist 1950s and the emergence from the poverty resultant from that isolationism are both central to the issues being presented here. In *Exposure* we are shown the effect of the demise of the agricultural economy in the increasingly depopulated west: the snooping, spying old landlady sitting in contemptuous judgment of the foreigner and the Dublinmen while taking salacious pleasure from her eavesdropping as the men act out their fear of and contempt for women, in the person of the French photographer. In *Criminal Conversation* we are shown the society which has replaced the old rural one, as people migrated from the farms to the cities, in all its vacuous desperation. Although he rigidly refrains from the polemical, Hickey is clearly identifying an inadequacy in modern Irish society and in doing so inviting its members to address the problem. The implication here is that the very core of its sexual attitude may be rotten--quite apart from the political wrangling over divorce and abortion--and the way in which Irish men and women relate to each other is a significant problem.

On another level, Hickey's next film represents a departure from the conflict between the genders. It is called *Attracta,* after the principal character, an unmarried elderly Protestant schoolteacher, and adapted from a William Trevor story by Trevor himself. Through a voice-over narrative, we learn that she was orphaned, her parents having been killed in the 1920s by the old IRA.

In a turnabout development, however, the persons responsible have looked after her since, and she seems to have forgiven them and found a way to carry on. Forgiveness is the theme here, and Attracta teaches it fervently. She teaches about the woman who received the severed head of her lover in the post and the evils of conflict. Finally, she learns of a woman who is raped by paramilitaries and subsequently kills herself--this is more than she can take, and marks the beginning of her descent into insanity. She seems to take on the pain of others as though it were her own, and the burden drives her out of her mind.

As in *Exposure* and *Criminal Conversation,* a woman is again victimized here. The violent conflict of the old IRA and the Provos is again (as in *Maeve* and *Anne Devlin* and even in *The Crying Game*) presented as a predominantly masculine proclivity. Attracta is a metaphorical woman: the ultimate nurturer, taking on herself the burden of all the pain and horror of that violence. She asks herself if she failed somehow to teach forgiveness urgently enough, if she could have done more to prevent the killing.

Through the narrative--the first-person expression of this concern--the character is asking the audience if they have done enough too. It amounts to a powerful statement of moral responsibility and of the trap that is the denial of evil--that we are condemned to repeat our mistakes if we fail to learn from them.

Stylistically, this film is much closer to its subject than Hickey's previous work. Although she is finally driven mad, and though

Attracta is presented as a victim, she is also a martyr and a symbol of ultimate good. In this film, we are allowed to get close to the subject, to understand her pain and suffering in a way that we were not allowed in *Criminal Conversation.*

The Television Films of Pat O'Connor

Continuing the theme of woman's lot in Irish society in another context is Pat O'Connor's film of yet another William Trevor story, *The Ballroom of Romance.* This was produced by RTE and the BBC in 1982, and aired by both networks. It was a high-budget production relative to RTE product of the time, and though intentionally scruffy-looking, the film is quite lavish in its level of detail, period atmosphere (set in the 1950s), and cinematic quality. It is also peopled with some of the best acting talent in Ireland at the time, including Cyril Cusack, Brenda Fricker, Anita Reeves, and the great actors John Kavanagh and Mick Lally.

The film follows Bridie (Fricker) as she prepares for and goes to the weekly dance at the Ballroom, run by Mr. Dwyer (Cusack). It is a bleak, dusty country hall with a bandstand at one end and a cloakroom at the other, and the crowd gathered there is plain, rough country folk, many of them approaching (or well into) middle age. The pattern is one that was typical of such gatherings: the men would congregate at a pub beforehand to bolster their courage, and take frequent breaks in the cloakroom for further nips of whiskey, waiting until the evening was nearly out before venturing among the women. On the opposite wall stand the women, notable among them being Bridie, who is somewhat older than the rest. The evening is interrupted by Mr. Dwyer making a speech about the Ballroom and all the marriages that have begun there--reading out letters from happy couples overseas, the alumni. This contrasts with the stark geometry of the two groupings within the hall, and the suspicion and mistrust with which these two sexually divided groups regard each other.

Bridie, we discover, has fancied Dano Ryan (Lally), but discovers that he is committed elsewhere and turns her attention to the edgy and offensive Bowser Egan (Kavanagh). They argue, the evening ends, and she leaves the hall. Bowser decides to go after her, but is waylaid by another woman (Reeves), whom he insults before walking out. The woman says, "What's she got that I haven't?" and Mrs. Dwyer, sweeping up nearby, replies, "Farmable land, maybe." O'Connor cuts to the road, where Bowser has caught up with Bridie and the pair are walking their bicycles along beside each other. He promises her that his mother will die soon and then they can marry; then he asks her into the field with him, presumably for sex. She goes, and the camera picks Bowser up again afterward as the sun is rising over the fields, taking another slug of whiskey from his flask as Bridie cycles away.

The irony in this piece, like *Exposure,* is in the title. The one thing that is utterly lacking from all the exchanges depicted is romance. We are shown lives which are bleak to the point of desperation and seemingly utterly loveless. This is a look back at the Ireland of the fifties which is devoid of any sentimental nostalgia at all; everyone in the piece is sad or despicable, or both at once (as in the case of Bowser). We are shown a society in decay, in which those who have achieved a measure of happiness have all gone elsewhere--and the implication is that the two things are closely connected.

Ballroom of Romance makes a strong statement to the Irish living in the cities and to those who have emigrated to other countries and may harbor nostalgic images of the Irish countryside by showing them the truly hard life many country people were forced to live, and the bleak nature of their relations to one another. Mrs. Dwyer's comment is central to the theme: many men in that time and that society were simply waiting for their parents to die so that they could take over the farm (the only thing any family possessed of any real value) and thus be in a position to marry. Frequently this didn't happen for many years, and the result was marriages between very old men and young women who were still of childbearing age. Doubtless, many of these matches were loveless ones, built upon hard economic reality rather than romance, and *Ballroom* stands as a portrait of the kind of desperation to which many of these people (particularly the women) were condemned.

In the following year, O'Connor directed the film version of Neil Jordan's short story *Night In Tunisia,* again for RTE. Again the theme was sexual, but this time a bit more upbeat, telling the story of an adolescent boy's growing sexuality one summer in a seaside resort. The boy is the son of an itinerant musician playing in one of the many showbands which were popular in Ireland in the 1950s, especially at such resorts. He becomes fixated upon a particularly attractive (and sexually indiscriminate) young woman in the town, while also dealing with his relationship to his father. *Night In Tunisia* deals neatly with the two-pronged dilemma of male maturity: how to deal with the emerging idea of women as sexual beings, and how to deal with other males having defined one's own sexuality. Jordan's script handles both neatly, using the saxophone as both a metaphor for sexuality and a device by which the boy and his father find common ground. The instrument would reappear later in *Angel* in a very different metaphor, and feature quite prominently in Roddy Doyle's *The Commitments* (the metaphor this time blending music and sex), in which the mouthpiece of the saxophone is compared to one of Kim Basinger's nipples.

Mark Kilroy: *Hard Shoulder*

Before RTE got out of the film sponsorship role, another significant television movie was made, which is appropriate to mention here. This was *Hard Shoulder,* written and directed by Mark Kilroy and produced by Jane Gogan, who had also produced Fergus Tighe's *Clash of the Ash.*

2. *Hard Shoulder*: **Johnny Murphy and his sales force head down the country to sell fire extinguishers.** (Courtesy of the Irish Film Archive and Mark Kilroy)

This was more of a mystery/adventure film, and an Irish "road" film, although not so starkly bleak as was *Traveller*. At the beginning, we're introduced to Ella (Olwen Fouere), who is in the process of finding new lodgings after her room in a boardinghouse has been robbed and ransacked. Then we cut to her waiting in a drab office to interview for a job, then to a group, including her and the sales manager Henshaw (Johnny Murphy), traveling out of Dublin to make a series of sales calls.

It turns out that they are selling stolen fire extinguishers, but they don't sell them very readily and several of the trainee salespeople drop out, leaving Ella, Henshaw, and a young man named Tony (Donal O'Kelly) to travel together. At night, Henshaw returns to Dublin and sets the warehouse on fire, returning the next morning to wake Tony and Ella. After further scenes of failed sales attempts in country towns, we see Henshaw arguing with someone on the phone. He is subsequently taken ill, and Tony drives him to a hospital.

Then the film turns into a chase: a carload of mysterious gangsters catches up to the two novices, and we learn the nature of the

mystery. They are the same ones who broke into Ella's room--it turns
out (rather improbably) that the head gangster is her father, from
whom she had been hiding.   After some permutations of the chase
(including a stop in a religious relic shop), and Henshaw's death in the
hospital, the pursuers corner Ella and take her to a country road to
meet her father. A heated exchange follows, and she pulls a gun from
the car's glove box and shoots him.   She walks away down the road,
Tony hitches a lift back to Dublin, and the credits roll.

Belabored though it is with some rather hard-to-believe plot
devices, this film still succeeds in establishing a convincingly dreary
washed-out atmosphere by means of which it paints a picture of
alienation within one's own culture. All the protagonists seem to be at
loose ends: either running from something or lacking a sense of
purpose (i.e., a job). They are all somehow expectant that this venture
will help correct that, but we, of course, know differently. The film
spirals down into increasing depths of desperation and contempt and
never allows a note of relief. The Dubliners are utterly out of place
outside their own culture, and are treated (rightly, as it turns out) with
suspicion and contempt by the country people.   Henshaw is
unceremoniously dismissed from one of his sales calls with the
pejorative epithet, "You Jackeen scut!" (There is no more vehement
expression of contempt for Dubliners in Irish slang.)
      Apart from the cultural split between country folk and city
dwellers (akin to the split between travelers and settled people we'll
see in Joe Comerford's film, *Traveller*), there is a clearly defined
separation between generations. Ella and Tony are somewhat allied to
each other in outlook and mores, as Henshaw is with her gangster
father.   Her action in shooting her father may be symbolic of the
rejection of the old culture by the young (as we will also see in Fergus
Tighe's *Clash of the Ash*), but this film just drops it there--we get no
hint of a direction in which the young people will go.
      Compared with the early work of Neil Jordan or that of Kieran
Hickey, *Hard Shoulder* seems to need more structure to its story and a
firmer grasp of both character and metaphor.   Still, it's a good mood

piece and a brave attempt to deal with the alienation within Irish society in the 1980s, a theme that would occupy much of the work of Roddy Doyle several years later. Incidentally, Johnny Murphy (who would later play the cop in Cathal Black's *Pigs*) was to achieve his greatest exposure as Joey "The Lips" Fagan in Doyle's *The Commitments*.

The Television Work of Roddy Doyle

As a writer of films, Roddy Doyle came into the medium without really intending to. He had set out to be a novelist, but after a few playscripts and a successful start to a career as a prose writer, Doyle had *The Commitments,* which turned out to be one of the most successful films about Ireland in recent history. We'll deal with that film in chapter eight, but there have been two subsequent projects written by him and produced for television that are well worth discussing here.

The first of these, *The Snapper,* was originally produced for the BBC and was later reedited and released as a feature, largely on the strength of *The Commitments.* In fact, it was the second in a trilogy of novels, all revolving around the Rabbitte family of Barrytown (a fictional estate in North Dublin), which dealt with specific aspects of contemporary Irish culture in a realistic way tinged with understanding and sympathy. (For *The Snapper,* the name of the family was changed from the novel because of contractual arrangements with the company which had produced *The Commitments.*) Doyle had already managed to capture the mix of cynicism, optimism, and hooliganism which is very much a part of Dublin's male culture; what he attempted with *The Snapper* was to portray the tenacity and dignity of a Dublin girl who has been caught in a double compromise. Her secret, of course, is that she's pregnant. That doesn't remain a secret long, but even the humiliation of that pales next to the identity of the "snapper's" father--a rather flabby, whining older man from across the road with whom she had sex one night in an alcoholic daze.   The film is about the maturation of the girl, Sharon, into a woman who must deal with the consequence of an adolescent mistake--but it is equally about the maturation of her father, who must come to terms with the shame he feels and his conflicting feelings of love and protectiveness.

There are, in fact, a number of conflicts and contradictions at work: the girls who are Sharon's friends and bar-mates (as in *The Commitments*) take unwed pregnancy as routine, and the males in the same pubs sip away at their pints and talk of their own sexual exploits. Nonetheless, when Sharon becomes pregnant, she is ostracized by these same people, and her father is made the butt of his friends' humor. In the end, they come to depend upon each other--father and daughter--and the "snapper" serves as a rallying point for Rabbitte family solidarity. Like the other two stories in this trilogy (there are plans for a film of the third novel, *The Van*), this one ends on an upbeat, if bittersweet note; there resides in most of Doyle's work a faith in the essential strength and goodness of the working-class Irish, a goodness that is not rooted in religious faith necessarily, nor in airy notions of Celtic myth, but in the simple sense of fair play practiced by the decent, hardworking people who have long inhabited the poorer housing estates of Dublin.

On the strength of *The Snapper,* the BBC produced another television series written by Doyle and based in a similar family situation. This was entitled *Family* and, though recut for feature release, has not received extensive distribution. It may be that it was too long to reduce to cinema-length without decimating the plot (it ran four hours on television), or it may be that, unlike the Barrytown trilogy stories, this one lacks the refreshing note of optimism. Although *Family* was aired on both the BBC and RTE, it was essentially a BBC project, and it raised some hackles in Ireland. The story revolves around a poor, working-class family who live in a Corporation housing block (a state-subsidized housing project). These structures are to be found in many areas of Dublin, and they look like welfare housing anywhere does: concrete-slab construction, flimsy doors and plain walls covered with graffiti, and grounds littered with dog feces and scraps of paper and plastic.

Essentially, *Family* deals with the process by which Paula, a wife and mother, casts herself and her children free from the abusive presence of her husband, Charlo. Here again, we have the picture of the Irish male trapped in some sort of delayed adolescence: self-indulgent, temperamental, and irresponsible. Unlike Jimmy Rabbitte Sr., however, Charlo lacks the endearing side to the personality and he lacks the intellect that has proved the redeeming feature of some of Doyle's other male characters. Charlo crosses the line when he makes sexual advances to his own daughter, and it is at this point that Paula throws him out of the house and decides to go it alone. The story then follows her trials: friends of Charlo's making sexual overtures to her, difficulties finding work to pay the rent, difficulties dealing with the children. As time passes, more and more things go wrong in her life, and she falls further into desperation. Then, near the end, Charlo makes an attempt to get back into the house and, though Paula weakens momentarily, she does rebuff him with finality; we know then that he won't be back and that she is utterly on her own and in charge of her own life.

But it isn't much of a life: she has three children she can barely feed, rent she can hardly afford, and a dead-end job cleaning offices late at night. (Earlier, we were shown a scene in which she abruptly quit work as a housecleaner for a wealthy business couple in which the breadth of the gulf between rich and poor in the new class order of Irish society was very sharply drawn.) On top of that, it is becoming apparent that the damage done by Charlo to their elder son will likely be irreparable; the child is a virtual carbon-copy of his father, and we're given little reason to suppose that he will grow into any other sort of adult. Doyle leaves us with a small joke, but one that really only accentuates the despair. As Paula has insisted that the family sit down to a meal together and finished a prayer over it in which God is thanked for the "bounty set before us," the smallest child looks up and replies, "But I don't *like* bounty!"

Family was shown in the summer of 1994; as a BBC production with some small support from RTE, it may stand as the last example of RTE's nonparticipation in film production. Since the reorganization of the Film Board and the removal of the revenue cap from RTE, the first round of FilmBase/RTE short film awards has been given out and those projects are under way. From a close involvement with the film community, both in-house and under freelance contract, the Irish television entity had virtually vanished. Now it appears to be back with a vengeance (and a budget) and hopes are high for a new alliance between the indigenous film community and the most likely and appropriate buyer and distributor of its product. There are still many doubts to be quelled and questions answered: To what extent will RTE censor that product? How much will commercial constraints dictate content? How much political influence might be brought to bear on these projects?

There is certainly a sense of guarded optimism in these quarters; it seems as though the government has decided to deal with film in a new way and it has enlisted the aid of the largest single producer of audiovisual product in Ireland to assist. These are pivotal actions and pivotal times, and the changing political and cultural climate of the whole nation does seem to bode well for a continuation of the much-touted Irish filmmaking "boom."

Notes

1. Quoted by Kevin Rockett in "Culture, Industry, and Irish Cinema," in *Border Crossings: Cinema in Ireland, Britain, and Europe*, John Hill, Martin McLoone, and Paul Hainsworth, eds. (Belfast/London: Institute for Irish Studies/British Film Institute, 1994): 126.

CHAPTER FOUR
CENSORSHIP

In chapter 1, I mentioned the tradition of film censorship which has been a fact of life in Ireland almost since the first films were shown there. It is significant that, though the individuals in power from one government to another and the ideas espoused by them may have been diametrically opposed, the need to control the images and ideas contained in film and broadcast media represents a continuum across those political changes.

As it has in other countries, the original impetus for censorship in Ireland had as its root the desire to protect public sensibilities from alien (and presumably seditious) ideas. In the early years of this century, the Canadian director Sidney Olcott was actively making a series of cheap and quickly produced dramatic films on Irish themes for the United States market. Many of these were historical in nature, some based upon the Irish plays of Dion Boucicault, the famous melodramatist of the late nineteenth century and a Dublinman of mixed Irish-French parentage. (Boucicault was also famous for his plagiarism and embellishment, so the truth about his origins is still in some doubt.) Olcott worked from around 1907 into the 1920s, and managed to offend the sensibilities of both the Catholic Church and the British government at the same time. He was blasted from the pulpit and spied upon by the agents of Dublin Castle (the seat of British power in Ireland at that time).[1]

Though Olcott probably didn't know it then, he had established a pattern for the relationship between government and filmmakers that persisted, in varying degrees of intensity, into the last decades of the century as well. 1921 saw the formation of the Irish Free State and the withdrawal of British military and direct governmental control, and the outbreak of civil war between the two factions of the republican movement. The war ended in the following year, and the year after that (1923) the Censorship of Films Act was written into law. If we take into consideration the tight control exercised by British authority in Ireland prior to the establishment of the Free State, it is true to say that the Civil War years were virtually the only ones in which the country was free of film censorship.

Apart from being enacted with remarkable haste, the censorship system is also remarkable in the autonomy it gives to the censor himself and in the broad powers bestowed by it:

> The censor is left almost entirely to his own discretion, Clause 7 (2),
> (4) empowering him to reject a complete picture or require cuts to
> be made in a picture according as he is of the opinion that such
> picture or some part thereof is unfit for general exhibition in public
> by reason of its being indecent, obscene, or blasphemous, or because
> the exhibition thereof in public would tend to inculcate principles
> contrary to public morality or would be otherwise subversive of
> public morality.[2]

Historically, little attention has been paid to the qualifications (or lack thereof) ascribed to the individual who functioned in this capacity to make such critical decisions. As Ciaran Carty noted in *Film Directions*,[3] "Apparently the first film censor, James Montgomery, on being asked in 1923 what he knew about movies, replied: 'Nothing, but I know the Ten Commandments.'" The tenor of Montgomery's tenure was to set the pattern for the attitude held by subsequent censors toward their job--a particularly significant thing, given the virtually unlimited powers bestowed thereon.

To understand this, it is important to visualize the process of censorship. A potential exhibitor of a film brings a print to the censor, and after paying a fairly hefty fee for the privilege, is given a list of objectionable particulars: shots that must be cut, scenes excised, changes made to a film's title, or complete denial of the right to show the piece. Once the alterations have been made, the film is issued a certificate for exhibition and may be shown.

There is an appeal process by which the exhibitor may get another hearing. Any cinema operator who feels unfairly dealt with by the censor may take the case to a review board to have it reconsidered. Notably, however, it has been a tradition that the review panel consist of two members of the clergy, one Catholic and one Protestant. We may reasonably surmise that reversals of the censor's decisions are rather rare occurrences, given the criteria upon which the films are being assessed.

We can, however, only surmise because the proceedings of the censorship process are officially categorized as confidential under the Official Secrets Act and may not be made public. Hence it is that Carty was also able to say with complete accuracy:

> Although cabinet papers dealing with Mr. de Valera's Government during World War II are available for scrutiny in the Public Records, information about whether or not a Laurel and Hardy movie might have been cut in the 1920's is deemed too sensitive to divulge.[4]

So, in practice, the details of the censorship process are officially and legally reckoned to be a confidential transaction between the censor and the exhibitor, and no one outside the government is privy to them. The audiences for films and the general populace, as constituents of the government, have been carefully excluded from the legal mechanism whereby the content of films they are to be allowed to see is controlled. And though the justification for this system is built upon the altar of public morality, it is only fair to say that there is also a political agenda interleaved within it that has proven beneficial to governments in the past.

The political need to control the portrayal of Irish images has its roots in the delicate political balance of the Free State and all of the governments of the successor Republic. Immediately following the War of Independence (which resulted in the withdrawal of the official British presence) the two factions of the republican movement fell out in disagreement over the structure of the new government.

(Essentially, the conflict was between the acceptance of the treaty which set up the Free State and remained tacitly within the British Empire and the ideal, which was to press on with military action until an independent republic was established. In the event, the Free State evolved into the Republic anyway, and the ideal was achieved, except in the North.) In essence, these factions evolved into the two dominant political parties, Fianna Fail and Fine Gael: the former embraced the left-leaning republican ideology, and the latter the more conservative view of the Free Staters. In the modern political climate the political differences are negligible, but in the 1920s, they were powerful and emotionally charged, and tinged with the animosities of personal hatred that any civil war must breed.

The political victors in the post-civil war era were de Valera and his party, the Fianna Fail. Although officially supportive of the old IRA and its aim of independent status outside the Empire and reunification with the North, de Valera moved into the Free State government and transformed it into the Republic by a combination of political sleight of hand and sheer force of will. This put his government in an awkward position politically: they had, at one point or another, stood on both sides of the fence as regards the loyalties left from the civil war, and the result has been that those issues have never really been resolved. They managed to impose peace on the population, but the mechanism was the establishment of a dominant single-party government that often looked rather like a dictatorship (and was called such by de Valera's opponents) and carefully controlled the flow of ideas to the populus as regarded politics and history. The de Valera government carefully built its agrarian idyll as a positive goal to place before its people, and ruthlessly suppressed any ideas which ran counter to that or questioned the version of history espoused by that government. Joe Comerford again:

> The situation was that there was civil war in Ireland--first there was the Rising in 1916 and the Civil War in the early twenties--but the Civil War has never ended, it's gone underground. (It's not like the Spanish Civil War which became a massive conflict and actually was, to a great extent, resolved.) And over certain periods it

re-emerged; it hasn't absolutely exploded, but there's the potential. You know, the first move into Irish censorship was by the Catholic Church, and the controlling of censorship was what they did. And when you had the State moving in you really put fear in, because all the natural prerequisites to develop a film culture were there. It wasn't really poverty (although the country was poor), it was a deliberate move not to develop film, in my opinion, because the political center--the status quo--was afraid of the potential. The psyche of the people seemed too fragile to reflect on itself in film or to deal with how the State came into being.[5]

There were, in addition, a number of tendencies over the years that lent a decided bias to the process. In general, the censors and members of the Appeals Board were inclined to a more conservative view, both morally and politically. They perceived themselves as defenders of the public mores against outside invasions (the film product of other countries at times characterized as "filth, dirt, and distortion") and against political ideology that may have been opposed to that of the government or Church. Dr. Richard Hayes, successor to Montgomery (and therefore Ireland's second film censor), was publicly quoted as saying, "anything advocating Communism or presenting it in an unduly favourable light gets the knife."

Adding to this political and moral conservatism was the fact that prior to the 1970 amendment of the censorship laws, there were no certificates denoting age restrictions on admission to specific films. Therefore, any film not deemed to be suitable for viewing by the youngest children was banned from presentation to anyone. This had its legal basis in the constitutional enshrinement of the family under law; a clause that also legally defined the woman's place in society as a domestic. Subsequent to that, there has been provision to certify a specific film for showing to limited audiences of a particular minimum age, and this has gone a long way toward opening the field of possibility. During the "general certificate" years, over 3,000 films were banned altogether and over 8,000 cut prior to release.

Despite his connections with the entertainment industry and the more liberal attitude exhibited during his reign (as opposed to that of Dermot Breen, who preceded him), Frank Hall apparently still regarded himself as a guardian of public morality and seemed intent upon upholding the rather conservative line of thought traditionally associated with the film censor. So, while Breen's record in office shows about 25 percent of films submitted refused certificates, Hall's ran roughly half that. History, however, remembers Hall for his refusal to certify *Life of Brian* for Irish release, presumably under pressure from Catholic Church authorities who regarded it as blasphemous.

Although the censorship law was framed in terms that mitigated against any sort of free expression, it has recently shown signs of suffering from its age. It is doubtful whether such a law could be brought into being today, and both the moral/political climate which permitted it to be drafted and the technological circumstances which were assumed in its operational structure have changed sufficiently to assure the Irish film afficionado that he or she may see virtually any film in its uncut version simply by engaging in one of several simple subterfuges.

Notable among these was the Irish Film Theatre, formerly located in Stephen's Green. The IFT was a film *club* rather than a cinema for general admission, and one simply bought a membership rather than a ticket. As the censor's brief pertained to public showings, any private film club could show a film without having to acquire a certificate. Thus it was that many films which had failed to pass the censor's scrutiny were still shown in Dublin at the IFT.

The IFT no longer exists, but its mission has fallen to the new Irish Film Centre in Dame Street. The IFC is a subordinate entity to the Film Institute of Ireland, and is housed in a courtyard behind the Friends' Meeting Hall at the corner of Dame and Eustace Streets on Dublin's south side. It is quite well designed, upmarket and trendy (with its own bar/restaurant); an attractive place to be and a flattering venue for the screening of Irish filmmakers' work as well as the work of many people from other countries. Oddly, this is the fruit (at least in part) of government funding, making it possible to view films which were denied permission for general release by one branch of the government by virtue of financial support provided by another branch. (As hopeful as this may make things look, however, it is true that the

IFC's plans to screen *Natural Born Killers* in April 1995 were thwarted by a barring order from the Department of Justice.)

This is illustrative of the fundamental dichotomy at work in the apparently contradictory behavior of the Irish government toward films and filmmakers: the bureaucrats have had great difficulty deciding how to categorize cinema. At times it has been viewed as a propaganda tool with which to shape public opinion or as an industry with the potential to create jobs for Irish workers. At other times it was characterized as a threat to the political and moral security of Irish life from a corrupt Anglo-American culture, and (much more rarely) it has been treated as a legitimate form of artistry and self-expression. It is to the credit of the IFT and the successor IFC that the last view has been kept alive.

It is also to the credit of the current film censor, Sheamus Smith, that the aesthetic merits of a film under consideration for certification have become a major factor in that consideration. Smith has been something of a breath of fresh air in the stale rooms of the censor's office in Harcourt Terrace. As Shane Barry has noted,[6] the offices of the new censor more closely resemble those of an upmarket film distributor, walls lined with film posters and a friendly and efficient staff. The office has come rather a long way since the days of Montgomery, both in atmosphere and in sophistication and understanding of the film craft.

This is because Sheamus Smith actually made a living as a film producer; he is the first Irish film censor to have been so intimately acquainted with the craft and the industry. He has worked in several markets and in many capacities, and has achieved a thoroughgoing familiarity with the process of filmmaking, its artistic merits and pitfalls, and the difficulties encountered by Ireland's indigenous filmmakers. Smith learned his trade in North America, returning to Ireland from a stint at Disney in 1961. He produced commercials for RTE for a number of years, leaving to take over the National Film Studios (Ardmore) in 1975, along with John Boorman. When the NFSI were closed in 1982, he went freelance, producing film pieces largely for television distribution. Since 1986 he has been the film censor, although continuing to produce a few projects as well.

Not surprisingly, the record of the office has been shown to be substantially more liberal since Smith took charge. Of the 172 films submitted in the last year of his predecessor's tenure, 18 were ordered cut and one rejected. By contrast, of 153 submitted in the next year--Smith's first year--seven were cut and none rejected. In 1989 and 1992, none were cut or rejected, and the figure for each category since 1987 has been two or fewer.[7]

Smith did refuse certification to *Natural Born Killers*, citing arguments against any redeeming aesthetic value. There have been a number of appeals during his tenure, but these have mainly been objections raised by distributors over age limitations imposed on their films rather than instructions to ban or cut them. Smith has made it clear that he respects the integrity of the filmmakers, and doesn't want to presume to cut their work himself or to encourage film distributors to do so either. This is, by comparison to his predecessors, unprecedented enlightenment, and must be responsible (at least in part) for the expansion in numbers of screens available to Irish audiences and the variety and timeliness of the films being shown on them.

But there is another means of circumvention of the censorship law, one which owes its existence to the development of new technology. It was, of course, beyond the wildest imaginings of the bureaucrats of 1923 to think that television would ever exist, never mind become the pervasive instrument of entertainment that it is today. Even videotape recording was not a reality until the late 1950s, so the infiltration of the VCR into virtually every household must have come as a shock and a surprise to those who would control what people can see. Nonetheless, the VCR has invaded Ireland, and with it the video rental shop, so it is now possible to acquire virtually any film in its original form if one is willing to watch it on a small screen. As the video aftermarket has impacted upon the audience for cinematic film releases, so has it reduced the influence of the film censors; indeed, the banning or cutting of a film on cinematic release probably increases the demand for it when it becomes available on videotape. This twist in the marketing reality has necessarily reduced, in some measure, the power of the censor, and its combination with the person of a sympathetic individual in the censor's office has worked to make the menu available to the film audience in Ireland infinitely more varied than it was only twenty years ago.

Still, the advent of broadcast television with the establishment of Telefis Eireann (later Radio Telefis Eireann) in 1960 began to open up this chink in the armor of the censor's brief much earlier. Ireland had a radio network for many years, but in 1960 it was felt that home-produced television was also desirable. While British TV could be received in the eastern and northern areas of the country, those in the western and southern reaches have been reliant on RTE, and thus the mission to supply them with television programming could also be combined with the desirable ability to control the content of that programming. As well, the old moral superiority bias was in play: though Dubliners could get "Coronation Street," it was popularly seen as tangible evidence of the inferior moral/spiritual state of English culture, in light of which Irish programming could be strictly censored and not suffer appreciably by comparison.

Thus it was that, while RTE was governed by the Ministry for Posts and Telegraphs and thus not subject to the dictum of the film censor, the post of film censor for television was created in-house in order that the on-air product be seen to have been vetted for wholesomeness of content before being broadcast to the nation.

Interestingly, the person selected for the job was none other than Liam O'Leary, certainly the preeminent scholar of Irish film at the time, and quite a vocal advocate for the indigenous film community. Among the members of that community, he has achieved something of the status of a hero and a sage. O'Leary worked for some time in the National Film Archive in London, where he discovered prints of films made in Ireland in the early years of the century. Returning to Ireland, he began to campaign for the establishment of an Irish film archive, and to work tirelessly researching and writing about the history of Irish filmmaking. He died, unfortunately, before writing his three-volume history. But his presence as the film censor for Irish television further strengthened the notion, in an official way, of film as an aesthetic subject rather than a propagandistic one.

Also, while English television had been virtually uncensored through the 1960s (relative to Irish TV), the reignition of violent conflict in the North resulted in a clampdown on the British channels. Because of the outlaw status of the Provisional IRA *in Ireland*[8] a political censorship act called Section 31 was enforced, which prevented spokespeople for any outlawed organization from appearing on Irish TV. (This included Gerry Adams and any members of the IRA, INLA, etc.) The BBC instituted a "selective treatment" policy beginning in 1969 that allowed, in theory, for appearance by members of those organizations but was entirely discretionary in its application, rather like Ireland's film censorship law. Thus it was that under the government of Margaret Thatcher, virtually none of the nationalist spokespeople were granted airtime, and in 1981 the BBC banned the music video made for the song "Invisible Sun" by the rock band The Police, because it showed unacceptable images of violence by British troops in Northern Ireland.

Notwithstanding, the onslaught of new technologies has been relentless, and there is now direct-to-dish satellite television all over Europe. The efforts made over the years to control the content of cinematic imagery shown to the Irish people have thus come to little or nothing: the requirement of certification for public showing of films and the establishment of a national television network also censored (albeit much more loosely) for content have given way to virtually unlimited access to pictures and ideas for anyone with the price of a satellite dish.

All these things would seem to mitigate against the effectiveness of any sort of censorship; the new technology would seem to permit a virtually unrestricted forum for cinematic expression on the small screen, at least in theory. It is true that the existence of the Internet has provided just such a forum for verbal expression, and many governments (including the American) are trying, belatedly and ineptly, to impose some sort of content controls. Still, for the true film buff, there is no substitute for the big screen with its attendant audio quality and the social experience it entails. For many people, these things are important--the health of the film industry worldwide stands as testament to that. To those who make films, the medium is unlike any other; videotape has many unfortunate visual, format, and technical limitations which make it a poor second choice to film, if one is concerned primarily for the aesthetic. Thus it is that for many in Ireland, the presence of a censor is offensive. The secrecy within which the film censor is permitted to operate, the vagueness of the censor's powers, and the excessive influence of the clergy in the process of censorship are all aspects of the system which grate upon the sensibilities of many who make films and who appreciate filmmaking.   They may not favor the elimination of censorship entirely; the sense is that the subject should be open for discussion, based much more substantially upon the artistic merits of a given film, and essentially a civilian process much less influenced by religious and political biases.   As it stands now, there is nothing in the law which has changed: if the present censor leaves office, the content of films shown in Irish cinemas will still be subject to the whim and personal prejudice of his successor, and the results could thus be quite damaging.

Notes

1. Discussed in chapter 1 of *Cinema and Ireland.*

2. John Gerrard, "Irish Censorship--or Fighting for a Cleaner Cinema," *Sight and Sound* (Summer 1949): 81.

3. Ciaran Carty, "Confessions of a Sewer Rat," *Film Directions,* vol. 3, no. 9 (February 1980): 16-19.

4. Carty, 16.

5. Author's interview with Joe Comerford, June 1994.

6. Shane Barry, "Who's Protecting Who?" *Film Ireland,* vol. 44

(December 1994/January 1995): 16.

    7. Barry, 16.

    8. Since the Irish Civil War, the IRA has been an illegal organization within the Republic of Ireland. It is often mistakenly assumed (especially in the United States) that the government of the Republic supports the actions of the Provisional IRA in the North, probably because the IRA has adopted the tricolor of the Republic as its own banner.

CHAPTER FIVE
BREAKING THE MOLD

In the last twenty years or so, there has arisen a small corps of independent filmmakers, each with something particular to say. In many cases, this has entailed the confrontation of ideas that various people and organizations in Ireland would have preferred to have left alone.

This is not to say that every independent has had uncomfortable things to say, nor that each of those who has done so has always been confrontational. Notable among those who have made a singular reputation as independents, but not stirred things up to do so, has been David Shaw-Smith, whose *Hands* series carefully documented the skills of traditional artisans all over Ireland. Trained in Radio Telefis Eireann, Shaw-Smith made his name as a solid documentarist with an eye for texture, an ability to light and compose beautifully, and a relaxed way of presenting subject matter. Much of his work was done on commission from RTE, and has been shown on television in numerous countries.

His work has been resolutely upbeat and nonconfrontational in the manner of Eamon de Buitlear and his mentor, Gerrit van Gelderen, and though the authorities in Ireland might have preferred that all its indigenous filmmakers produced work of this kind, and though such films serve a very laudable purpose (especially in the preservation of aspects of Irish culture which are threatened with extinction), it was inevitable that people with more politically difficult things to say would get hold of film equipment.

Bob Quinn: *Caoineadh Airt Ui Laoire*

One of the earliest of these was Bob Quinn. Quinn is a Gaelic speaker and proponent of Gaelic culture who discovered early on that a safe haven and fertile base of operation was the Gaeltacht. The Gaeltachts are areas of the country in which native speakers of Irish Gaelic still live and use the old language in their daily lives. In an effort to preserve the old culture, the government made reservations of these areas, with monetary incentives to encourage the inhabitants to continue to use the old language and customs and to remain in the Gaeltachts rather than emigrate to the urban areas or abroad. This scheme has slowed the deterioration and emigration, but neither stopped nor reversed them, as was hoped.

The largest Gaeltacht was in Connemara, generally centered on Galway, and the most firmly held area was the Aran Islands. Linked with the mainland only by boat and the occasional aircraft, the Arans were well insulated from outside culture and the English language. This was the region featured in Flaherty's film (*Man of Aran*), and remained a stalwart outpost until the advent of direct-from-satellite TV reception in the last decade. There is now little that can be done to stop the incursion of English language and mainstream Anglo-American culture, although the government has launched a new television channel, Telefis na Gaeltachta, in the hope that provision of an Irish-language alternative will prove a popular option among the Islanders.

Bob Quinn was a refugee from Dublin, another ex-RTE employee, who moved to Connemara looking for freedom from the commercial constraints and censorship of the city. In 1972, he established his own film production company, Cinegael, originating on 16mm stock. Productions include *Caoineadh Airt Ui Laoire, Poitin, Atlantean, Budawanny,* and *The Bishop's Story.*

His first major project was a low-budget cinematic treatment of the famous Irish poem *Caoineadh Airt Ui Laoire (Lament for Art*

O'Leary). The poem tells the story of an Irish peasant who returns to Ireland from exile abroad a wealthy man and a military success. His presence is an embarrassment to the Anglo-Irish aristocracy, and his contentious nature brings him into conflict with a prominent landholder who kills him, ostensibly in a dispute over ownership of a horse. The story is, of itself, safely ensconced in the past and thereby not threatening to the status quo. What Quinn did with it, though, was to project it forward into the present day (1975).

3. *Caoineadh Airt Uí Laoire:* **Sean Ban Breathnach on horseback.** (Courtesy of the Irish Film Archive and Bob Quinn)

As told in the film, the story is a play-within-a-play. The film revolves around a theater group in the throes of rehearsal for a presentation of the poem in dramatized form. The director of the play is an Englishman, and Quinn sets him up almost immediately in conflict with his Irish cast. The Irish actors are playful, undisciplined, and a bit chaotic, while the director is the stereotypical stiff autocrat we expect him to be. The film then cuts back and forth between the past as represented by the story of the poem and the present as represented by the play rehearsal. As the pace of the intercutting accelerates, the parallels of the ancient and modern conflicts grow until they finally merge. The characters in both are rather broadly drawn, and the clear effort is to draw a picture of the essentially conflicting natures of the Irish and the English. The outcome is inevitable: the ancient conflict is reenacted and the statement made is quite blatantly anti-English.

What is unusual about this film, in the Irish context, is that it makes a fairly simplistic statement. The Irish people in it are consistently playful, uncomplicated, and resolutely clever--in short, childlike. There is a quality of innocence reminiscent of *Man of Aran* but without the relentless dirgelike plodding pace; rather, this film is a romp through the fields, which proves to be a powerful setup device for the shock of the inevitable violent resolution. The point made is entirely subjective, but all the more powerful for that: the Englishman as a symbol is shown to be the humorless oppressor and the Irish to be the playful innocents who are condescendingly abused and denigrated. This is not consistent with the "noble peasant" theme of the de Valera government propaganda, nor is it particularly palatable to the official position that bygones are better left behind and old animosities better let lie. The clear implication is that the essential quality of the Irish nature is incompatible with the culture of the English, and no note of compromise is sounded at all. The viewpoint of the filmmaker is also quite clear: that the Irish way of thinking and being is the more preferable of the two. The theme of separatism is quite strong, and in the context of its time (the reignition of the Troubles in Northern Ireland), the film may be taken to be a strong anti-British statement.

The atmosphere of *Airt Ui Laoire* strongly emphasizes the simplicity and cleverness of the bygone peasant culture and sets us up quite well for the harshness introduced into it by the foreign intruder. In this treatment, the victims are plainly the Irish and the victimizers the British. Nonetheless, there is the strong implication that the Irish have somehow achieved a deeper understanding of the things that are important, and that the British (both historically and in the person of the stage director) are doomed to wander about in a perpetual state of bewilderment brought on by the false assumption of cultural superiority. In this sense, Quinn has succeeded in making a fairly subtle statement about the conflict between British and Irish without resorting to the simpleminded railing and militancy into which such argument often deteriorates.

Tommy McArdle: *It's Handy When People Don't Die* and *The Kinkisha*

Historically, dating back to the melodrama of Dion Boucicault and perhaps beyond, there has been a genre of dramas such as these about the peasant culture and agrarian lifestyle of the old Irish, especially as it related to conflict with the British. Many of the strongholds of resistance were located in rural areas, and these have continued to be pockets of nationalist sentiment as well as serving as key elements in the nationalist mythology so carefully constructed in this century.

In this context, then, is an important film made in 1980 by Tommy McArdle and his twin brother, John. The film is called *It's Handy When People Don't Die*, which is a line from the film and a poignant statement of ironic impact. The central character in this film is also named Art, but this Art is a long way from the mythical war hero of the Bob Quinn film. Revolving around the Battle of Vinegar Hill, fought during the Rising of 1798, the film tells how the lives of people in a tiny village are altered by the effects of history and mythology.

It is important that the audience be familiar with this history, at least to the extent that they know that this battle was a rout for the Irish, who were armed only with pikes and pitchforks, and a sound victory for the well-armed and trained British troops. While the men of the village answer the call to arms and march off to the battleground, Art and the seanachie (storyteller) fall behind.

Eventually, they return to the village. Art hides himself on the fringes of the settlement, while the seanachie retreats to his cottage in the woods and locks himself in. Observing from his hiding places, Art watches the women and children digesting the importance of the events and the impact on their own, previously uncomplicated, lives. Taking pity on a woman (identified only as "The Brown Girl") whose lover has been reported killed, Art breaks his cover to sneak into the village and console her, but is unable to help. Her father is also reported killed, and she loses her sanity. The seanachie kills himself. Eventually, Art shows himself to the villagers, pretending that he's been to the battle and only returned to get a fresh horse. Excitedly, he describes the ferocity of the fighting, and invents a story of heroism and military victory by the Irish side. He then rides off, muttering the title line.

Of course, we know that the battle was a resounding defeat, and the questions posed by this film are those which plagued many of the Risings against the British down the years: why were the Irish never able to organize themselves into an effective military force (at least until this century), and what were the roles of cowardice, political division, and superstition in their failure to throw off their oppressor? As such, it spends much of its time and effort following Art around as he hides from the villagers and spies on them. Tommy McArdle has directed the film as an introspective piece, concerned mainly with the mind-set of this rather simple peasant who is forced to grapple with ideas and emotional conflicts well beyond anything he'd been accustomed to.

As such, it effectively contrasts the rather quiet, plain lives of simple farmers with the occasional violent (and seemingly mindlessly random) intrusion by the British soldiers. It is plain from the outset, in which a placid country evening is rudely and bloodily disrupted by those same soldiers, that the conflict inherent in the landscape is between rather pacific peasants and the greedy and violent intruders--and that, as regards capacity for violent brutality, the Irish will be outclassed. But the message in the film is principally directed at an Irish audience, and the portraits presented of the traditional village, as against those perpetuated in the modern Gaelic myth of Irish nationalism, are almost certain to rub the wrong way. Throughout, the motives and wisdom of the peasants' actions are questioned, and the mind-set of the protagonist is clearly not one of nobility nor selflessness nor devotion to the cause. The wisdom of male aggressiveness is also questioned, as its effects are played out among the women left behind, and the bravado that Art displays in the telling of his lie is clearly and strongly ironic, in view of the "noble peasant" mythology which has been constructed around this event and others like it. The inherent paganism of the peasantry is also clearly detailed (as it has been in the McArdles' other film, *The Kinkisha*).

Interestingly, when asked about the meaning of the film, Tommy stated that he had set out to make a study of the manner in which myths are made. This question (underlying all the other questions) is simply one of the frame of mind, personality, and circumstances surrounding the creation of a myth, especially as a contradiction of the historical facts. It may seem a bit extreme to take this point so literally, but we need only remind ourselves that Eamon de Valera referred to the Vinegar Hill battle when advocating violent overthrow of the British during a campaign speech in the 1920s, specifically admonishing the farmers gathered there to fight with pikes if they couldn't get guns. The mythology surrounding the various risings has been a powerful political tool in recent years, and the message in a film such as this would be quite powerful as well to an Irish audience familiar with that rhetoric.

The theme of paganism and superstition is one which forms the core of *The Kinkisha*, John and Tom McArdle's other film. Again relying on a familiarity with aspects of rural Irish culture, they have managed to portray modern-day people living with and using the technical trappings of post-Industrial Revolution society without having lost the vestiges of the old pre-Christian religion. As the preface to the film explains, a kinkisha is a child born at pentecost; such a child, according to the old belief, will be either a killer or the victim of murder unless its mother performs a ritual sacrifice to ward off the evil destiny. The ritual requires that she trap a robin and kill it, allowing the blood to drip onto the kinkisha. (McArdle says that this ritual is still practiced in some areas of the country.)

The mother (Margaret) and father (Ger; played by John McArdle) are a rather uncommunicative young rural couple, who are married by necessity.   The child born to them is the kinkisha, and the grandmother wastes no time in letting Margaret know what she must do. Margaret is somewhat resistant to the idea of such a sacrifice, and holds out until it becomes apparent that the child is troubled in some way. She speaks to the priest about the problem and is warned that the performance of a pagan ritual is a grave sin. Nonetheless, she decides to perform the rite and spends several days trapping the robin. Finally, she catches and kills the bird and anoints the baby, with assistance from the grandmother.

Much of the film is without dialogue, and McArdle takes full advantage of the scenes showing Margaret lying in wait for the robin to set the pace and mood of the piece. The effect is to describe the sort of person who, though living in the world of fact and reason, still maintains close contact with nature and the pagan beliefs and practices which were long indigenous to Ireland and helped to shape the character of its people. Despite the 1970s-trendy flared trousers and Rolling Stone haircuts, these people are shown to be rough and fairly elemental.   There is little communication and outward tenderness between Margaret and Ger, and he takes little or no interest in the care of the child. Their house is an old stone farm cottage, sparsely furnished, and their language and manner is both pragmatic and economical.

Their relationship to the priest (the only outsider depicted) is one of wariness--it is evident that he is not one of them, and his pronouncements are not really regarded as binding. The commission of the sin of pagan belief is taken rather lightly by the three principal characters, and though they try the various remedies mandated by modern society, it is the old way they turn to finally, and in which they place their faith. This dichotomy is nicely set up: the trappings of the 1970s, such as plastic buckets and hippie fashions, contrast pointedly with the whitewashed stone and muddy farmyard. Margaret finds herself in a marriage necessitated by pregnancy to a man she seems not to know very well, and with whom it seems things are not working out. In the end, she turns to ritual sacrifice both for her baby's well-being and to save her marriage, showing us that the trappings of late-twentieth-century culture, and even of Christianity, are mere surface dressing. Taken on a broader level, a statement is made here about the conflict between the indigenous Irish culture and the technocratic world which surrounds it, both in respect to the difficulty many Irish people have in relating to European and American culture and in respect to some of the ways in which the Irish are different and unique among the peoples of Europe.

Joe Comerford: *Traveller*

In much the same vein, and possessed of a strikingly similar atmosphere and character type is a film made in 1978 by Joe Comerford and scripted by Neil Jordan, *Traveller*. As with the preceding work, this requires that its audience be roughly familiar with a situation that exists in Ireland today, that of the traveling people. These are said to be the remnants of people who were dispossessed during the potato famine of the 1850s, and have since made a life on the roads, living like Gypsies, although completely Irish in their origins. For many years they would make their living repairing metalwork, and thus earned the name of "tinkers," a name which is now regarded as politically incorrect and slanderous. Since the repair of pots and pans is no longer lucrative, the travelers have resorted to whatever they could do to make money, tending toward casual labor and the sale of used car parts from their encampments by the roadside. There is hardly a part of the country which does not have them, and they are largely regarded with suspicion by the "settled" Irish in the belief that their main stock-in-trade is thievery.

The story of *Traveller* revolves around a young couple, Michael Connor and his very young bride, known only as "the Devine girl." The marriage is made by arrangement between their fathers, and the deal is struck in precisely the same way that the sale of a horse would be. As with *The Kinkisha,* these people say very little indeed and are quite cryptic when they do. The life they lead is shown to be relentlessly dismal and devoid of purpose; the wedding, which seems to be anything but a celebration of love, erupts into drunken brawling, and the young couple are confused, out of place, and uncomfortable whatever their surroundings.

All the characters have a quality of animalistic wariness about them, and their lives are suffused with a roughness and implied violence which must come from lives spent on the fringes of the larger (and predominant) society, as outcasts treated with suspicion and open hostility. The Devines seem to make their living trading in goods smuggled illegally across the border from Northern Ireland, as Devine gives the young couple some money and sends them into the North with his van to collect a consignment of television sets, presumably stolen. On the trip up they meet a man named Clicky, who travels some of the way with them. Their dealings with the man who sells them the television sets are much like those with their own people--wary and cryptic. On the return trip, they crash the van in a ditch and set off on foot. They then rob an old woman who runs a post office and go aimlessly on the run, staying in an abandoned house and a cheap seaside resort hotel. Finally, they are rescued by Clicky, who drives Michael to Devine's trailer (caravan) where Michael kills Devine. This is, apparently, retribution for Devine beating and perhaps raping his daughter, now Michael's wife. In the end, all three set off for England.

The theme which saturates *Traveller* is disaffection. No one seems ever to really engage anyone else, and it's something of a surprise when Michael shows his affection for his wife (if, indeed, that is the motive) by killing her father. There is a dullness about all these people that sets the tone; they behave in an animalistic way without any strong emotion or any sense of destiny. Everything they do seems to be motivated by a survival instinct, and their behavior is uniformly reactive to immediate needs: sex, survival, anger. The portrait painted here is mind-numbing and desperately depressing; virtually no redeeming qualities make themselves evident, and the characters' desperation simply deepens as they wander from one violent situation to another.

4. *Traveller:* **At "the Devine girl's" wedding.** (courtesy of the Irish Film Archive, the British Film Institute, and Joe Comerford)

Politically, this is a very hot potato. Although Ireland is free of racial discrimination, per se, the travelers represent a population which, though indigenous and deeply entrenched, is very much an outcast group and one which has been treated with contempt and neglect for many years. Only very recently have they begun to find a few articulate voices willing to speak on their behalf, and the open hostility toward them is only now beginning to ease. Because of their outcast status and their refusal to come off the road and settle in the community, the travelers' children have largely been left out of the school and health systems and are thus illiterate and often suffer from the effects of illnesses which could have been treated. They are

uniformly mistrustful of everyone outside their community, and are
fated from birth, in most instances, to a life of hand-to-mouth
existence and short-term expectations. For many years, they have
been swept under the rug or romanticized by the mainstream culture,
the result of which has been an inattention to the problem they
represent to Irish society and to their needs as legitimate residents of
the country.

The picture shown in this film is both desperate and difficult to
ignore: the clear statement here is that there is a sizable segment of
Irish society which is disenfranchised in its own country. The
oppressor here is no foreign invader, and the people being depicted
have done nothing except to be born into a tradition of poverty, flight,
and petty crime. While mainstream Irish society is busy chasing
economic success, it is occasionally reminded by some voice with a
social conscience that the travelers are still out there, their numbers
growing and their circumstances worsening. It ought to be no great
surprise that these voices are greeted with some distaste or ignored
altogether.

Pat Murphy: *Anne Devlin* and *Maeve*

Traveller is particularly important for another reason, though.
The creative forces exhibited therein would go on to make their marks
in very different, but no less important, ways. The script was written
by Neil Jordan, who has since made himself known internationally as
one of the high-profile Irish filmmakers, and it was directed by Joe
Comerford, who has made his name within the Irish independent film
community as the most prominent muckraker and maker of
"dangerous" films. The third person is Thaddeus O'Sullivan, whose
reputation as a director of photography in Ireland and England is
impeccable, and who has begun to build his portfolio as a director in
his own right. The hallmark of O'Sullivan's work is stunning, moody,

often breathtaking footage beautifully composed and lit, as evidenced in such films as Pat Murphy's *Anne Devlin* and his own *December Bride*.

Anne Devlin was the second feature-length project directed by Pat Murphy, in 1984. The woman referred to in the title was closely associated with Robert Emmet, who led the rebellion of 1803. The film is a marvelous period piece, very meticulously crafted and faithfully reproducing the detail and atmosphere of early nineteenth-century Ireland. It is also a strongly female film; the values represented and the point of view the director adopts are clearly those of a woman in a situation created and controlled by men.

Emmet, the legendary hero and leader of this Rising, is portrayed as an intellectual, well-educated Ascendancy sort (he was a Trinity College-trained Protestant) whose dedication to the cause of Irish independence and combination of leadership ability and penchant for careful strategic calculation make his an attractive persona to Anne Devlin on several planes. She comes from a family of sympathizers and participants of the republican cause and, by way of explanation, we are shown scenes in the beginning of the film of her father's incarceration and ill treatment at the hands of the British government. These scenes, which set up the principal action of the film, are carefully constructed and subtly underscore the sort of feigned subservience and thinly disguised animosity displayed by the Irish toward their conquerors, clearly illustrating the sort of quiet tenacity which permitted the Irish to sustain their hope and commitment to the possibility of ultimate release from occupation in the face of repeated defeats over the course of many centuries. It is also made clear that the qualities of patient endurance and dogged optimism which sustained the Irish independence movement throughout were ones which women, by virtue of the manner in which they have been treated by male-dominated society, were better adapted for and more accustomed to.

Having thus set up the context, both historically and personally, Murphy takes us into the Devlin/Emmet relationship. It is evident from their first meeting that Devlin is quite taken with Emmet, although it is not clear whether she is drawn to him because of a romantic attraction or out of more idealistic impulses. In any case, she is established as his "housekeeper," a cover for the fact that the house in which they live is really the military command post of the fledgling revolutionary army he commands. Their relationship is a bit prickly, neither sure of the other's role or place, until it becomes evident that Devlin is quite intelligent and has a strong tactical and organizational skill.

As we know from history the rebellion was crushed, as were many others before and since, but this film resolutely avoids dwelling on the military exploits of the men involved. Instead, we stay at the house with Anne Devlin and the other women, awaiting news of the outcome of the battle. Of course, the British soldiers arrive and arrest everyone, pausing to humiliate and abuse the women and children before hauling them off to prison.

It is at this point that Devlin's life takes a turn for the heroic. It is widely known or suspected by the British that she was Emmet's confidante, and she is tortured, starved, and locked in isolation.

The other participants in the revolt slowly succumb, and enough information is gathered to have Emmet hanged for his crimes against the State, but Anne never breaks. Always rather quiet and reserved (if intense), she retreats in her incarceration further into silence and finally into madness, but she never loses her devotion to Emmet and his cause, and never weakens. Eventually, she is released into civilian society again, but left impoverished and unacknowledged by the others in the movement for whom she sacrificed her sanity and much of her life.

Although tragic, the story is really about those noble qualities that Irish women have exhibited down the centuries: patience, devotion, and stamina. At no point in her trials does Devlin lose sight of her ideals or allow her personal devotion to flag, even though it is apparent that no one else is available or willing to give her support. Also, though the focus is on Devlin herself and therefore somewhat uplifting, the manner of her treatment by the other members of the republican movement is seen to be callous and self-serving. She, of course, stands as a painful and inconvenient reminder, to those who capitulated and incriminated Emmet, of their weakness and cowardice, but the indictment goes deeper than that. In the masculine world of revolution and violent political change, the heroism of an Anne Devlin was not acknowledged, and much of the point of this film has been the redressing of her grievance against subsequent historians and makers of the republican legend. As such, it stands as an eloquent and beautiful tribute without railing or proselytizing but rather presenting her story in a touching and tragic way, and encouraging us to empathize with her.

In some ways a stronger statement, because it is set in the Northern Ireland of the recent past, is Pat Murphy's earlier film, *Maeve.* This is the story of a woman from Belfast, now living as an expatriate in London. The story is told in flashback scenes and structured as a debate between Maeve and the men she had loved as a girl: her father and her republican boyfriend, Liam.

The conflict is occasioned by Maeve's return to Belfast from London, to which she had retreated from several kinds of violence and oppression. The film uses locales that may be significant to the Irish audience, such as the Giant's Causeway and Cave Hill, near Belfast. Scenery more familiar to the outside world, such as ruined buildings and streets fringed with razor wire and blocked by corrugated steel walls, places the action firmly in a war zone. These choices are very apt, considering the thesis of the piece--that the women of the North are victims of their own society (meaning the nationalist Catholic community), just as that society is victimized by the larger unionist community which controls the police and military forces.

Maeve makes the point, quite plainly, that the circumstances in which Northern Ireland's women find themselves are not likely to change significantly, regardless of the outcome of the military/political conflict. Thus it is that Maeve is able to deflect the hurt and annoyance expressed by Liam at her decision to leave him and move to London--living, as he sees it, among the enemy. For her, as an Irishwoman, there is more freedom in the relative anonymity of

London than within the tightly knit and invasive community in which she grew up. On her return home, she is seen to be at ease only with her mother, her sister, and her women friends in defiance of the landscape and historical context, both of which are redolent with the trappings of male-dominated violence. As Luke Gibbons notes in *Cinema and Ireland,*

> At the end of the film, Maeve comes to terms with her fractured identity by going on a drinking session with her sister and mother at the great antiquarian shrine of the Giant's Causeway, solidarity replacing community as they set their faces firmly against the landscape on their way home.[1]

This is, of course, akin to the argument Murphy made in *Anne Devlin,* that the republican movement and the conflict between it and the British/unionist forces is essentially male in character and has traditionally relegated women to the background or allowed them only subservient participation. The difference here is the documentary feel of the film and the underlying format of discussion and debate between Maeve and the two men in her life as to the meanings of their lives and the very different perspectives they must have due to the simple fact of differing gender and the fundamental difference in roles and viewpoints that it necessitates.

Like many other films made about the Northern Irish conflict by Irish filmmakers and directed for the Irish market rather than the sensationalist international market, *Maeve* doesn't pretend any solutions, simple or otherwise. What Pat Murphy has done is to characterize the situation in Northern Ireland--and describe how its politics have disenfranchised half of its constituents--and show us how one exponent of that situation has dealt with the personal conflicts arising out of her involvement with the situation and its people. The issues being addressed here are not those of politics and war, but rather the more subjective and emotive (and ultimately perhaps the more important) effects of political conflict on its victims. So, despite the use of the debate device to clarify the issues, and despite the somewhat documentary look of the film, this is really a more poetic statement about issues of emotion and psychological conflict than politics. A neat enough trick, and one that leaves us puzzled at its end and induces, perhaps, a more empathetic response than would a film which took a more objective point of view.

Fergus Tighe: *Clash of the Ash*

Pat Murphy has made only two films; it is indicative of the difficulty involved in financing independent projects and the lack of support from governmental resources in recent years that there are many people in the community of filmmakers who have made only two or three films despite a proven ability to make them well. Among these are two notable exponents of the disenfranchisement of the Irish male: Fergus Tighe and Cathal Black.

Tighe has made only one feature-length film, an introspective and highly subjective look at the plight of a young man in the southern reaches of the Republic entitled *Clash of the Ash*. Lest you be misled by the title's apparently violent tone, the reference is to the Irish national sport, hurling. The game is played with a hard cowhide ball much like a baseball and a stick made of ash called the hurley. The ball may be hit along the ground or through the air or "dribbled" down the field by juggling it on the spoon-shaped business end of the hurley. (Because the players traditionally wear no protection, there are few seasoned hurlers who still have their front teeth; it is a rough game.)

The film tells about a young man named Phil, who lives in Fermoy, in the northeastern part of County Cork. Phil is something of an outsider in his community, not really connecting with his family or friends. His one focus and fixation is hurling, and it occupies nearly all his time and thoughts. Failing his exams, he has no chance to go on to university and begins to drift further away from the people around him. He makes one tenuous romantic connection with a teenaged girl, but his relationships remain strained and superficial

with nearly everyone he knows. Finally, and impulsively, he quits the
hurling team in an argument with the coach. The presence of a
slightly older woman who has returned from living in London ignites
the spark in Phil's imagination, and he determines to set off for
London himself. His leavetaking is somewhat strained, and though
the ending is inconclusive and we suspect that he might not get on too
well in England, there is the slimmest note of increased understanding
between Phil and his father.

5. *Clash of the Ash:* **The mystique of the emigrant, returned from life in
London to the familiar confinement of the small country town.** (Courtesy of the Irish
Film Archive and Jane Gogan)

Fergus Tighe has addressed one of the serious social problems
affecting society in the Republic with this film. While not as dramatic
as the Troubles in the North, the rise of emigration being felt at the
time this film was made (1987) was again becoming a matter of
socio-economic concern and personal angst for many people. It had
been dealt with earlier, and in a similar treatment, by the playwright
Tom Murphy in his 1978 play, *A Crucial Week in the Life of a*

Grocer's Assistant.

In the stage play, this young man remains in his small village despite his contempt for the life there; in *Clash of the Ash*, the atmosphere of oppressive intrusion and the hopelessness of Phil's situation make his departure inevitable. What is different about this treatment is its reliance on visual tools to tell the story. While much Irish theater and film is dialogue-driven (as is *Maeve*), this film is reliant on clean shooting and smooth pace and structured in a simple linear way. This makes the bias more subjective, and we are concerned at the end with the resolution of Phil's internal conflict--to stay or to go--as a dilemma he must resolve in order to act. Phil stands as an example of the gulf which exists between generations in Irish society, a gulf which widened as the economy and the culture emerged into the mainstream of world culture. The conflict engendered is no less perplexing for Phil than for Maeve, and it is an equally subjective piece, albeit one whose structure is very different from the Murphy film. Like *Maeve, Clash of the Ash* leaves us with more questions than answers; the object is to stimulate feelings of introspection and perhaps to lead us to some empathy for and understanding of the dilemma in which Phil and his contemporaries find themselves.

At the end of *A Grocer's Assistant,* John Joe (the protagonist) spells out this problem to his parents:

> It isn't a case of staying or going. Forced to stay or forced to go. Never the freedom to decide and make the choice for ourselves. And then we're half-men here or half-men away, and how can we hope ever to do anything?[2]

This sense of disenfranchisement, of being something of an outcast in one's own community, may be indicative of the abrupt change of direction taken by Ireland in the 1970s and still under way. Under the anti-isolationist policies of the governments which succeeded de Valera's, the effort to be inward-looking and self-defining was turned on its head as Ireland reached out to Europe

and America for economic assistance. Of course, cultures like those
export lifestyle aspirations along with economic interaction, and the
comfortable (if limited) lives of the rural Irish were to be rather
profoundly altered by the change. The children who have grown to
maturity since this change began are faced with some very different
problems and questions than faced their parents, and they've been left
largely to their own devices to sort out their lives. Many have
emigrated to the United States, Australia, and England--not entirely
because of economic necessity, but partly to escape from the closed
culture and intrusive society of the small Irish village.

Cathal Black: *Pigs* and *Our Boys*

Some have only strayed as far as Dublin. This has the advantage
of permitting regular visits home but allowing the individual to carry
on in a much less restrictive lifestyle in the relative anonymity of the
city. The difficulty with this scenario is the fact that there has not
recently been much work to be found in Dublin, and some of those
who have relocated there have found themselves quite poorly off,
living in tenements or squats, frequently also abusing drugs. This is a
long, long way from the Gaelic idyll preached by the revivalists at the
turn of the century and enshrined by the early government of the
Republic. It is also the central theme of Cathal Black's wonderful
1984 film, *Pigs*.
    Jimmy Gibbons, the protagonist, is a homeless man who is also
the leader of a band of squatters who live in abandoned houses,
staying in one until they are forced to move on to another. At the start
of the film, we see Jimmy scouting for a new "squat," walking along
rows of old Georgian houses, many of which are boarded up or falling
apart. A number of the once-grand Georgian squares of central
Dublin were allowed to deteriorate, turning into slums and then
crumbling away, and it is in one of these moldy, drafty, and formerly

opulent houses that Jimmy finds a loose panel over a door and climbs in. Soon he has opened the place up, and the remainder of his brood of lost souls moves in as well.

These other "tenants" are a strange menagerie, and a sort of cross-section of society's outcasts. They include a prostitute and her pimp, a punk, a former mental patient (who is largely delusional) and an older man with a heart problem who goes to great lengths to look respectable and thereby preserve his dignity. Jimmy is evidently gay, a fact which earns him a beating at the hands of some of the punk's friends and makes his welfare claim--that he is supporting a wife--highly suspect. Together they manage to breathe some life into the old relic of a house, and in some ways the house becomes an important character too. This is another film shot by Thaddeus O'Sullivan, and he manages to make the squalid and creaky old building seem to have a life and a character of its own. The scenes are reminiscent of the etchings of the lives of Dublin's poor from the late nineteenth century and the more recent photographs of similar circumstances in the 1920s. As Luke Gibbons observes in *Cinema and Ireland,*[3] Black and O'Sullivan toe the line here, almost making the squalor seem picturesque and romantically appealing. But that may work in this film's favor. These Georgian houses have an innate elegance of form which shines through the layers of peeling wallpaper, dust, and cobwebs and offers both a sharp contrast between their original circumstances and their present ones and a slim ray of optimism that something of enduring value remains amid the rubble. Thus it is that, when the shabby band of misfits takes the place over and cleans it up (if only a little) and the windows are opened up to the light, we are led to believe that things might work out to their benefit in some way. Gradually, however, their band begins to fall apart and one by one they leave until finally only Jimmy is left. It's not long before the police, put on to him by the social worker whom he has been defrauding, come and take him away.

This is a film rife with potential for metaphor. Apart from depicting another aspect of Irish life that lives outside the stereotypes, Black seems to invite us to compare the band of confused outcasts, living in--but not part of--Dublin, and the Irish nation whose status as an emergent economy in the middle of western Europe and as a divided postcolonial nation also make it something of a misfit among the other English-speaking nations in the European community. Although not all the people in Jimmy's company are young, they represent certain types of characters whose presence in Irish society runs counter to the types and ideals embraced in the past by government and church. It can be difficult to be openly gay in Ireland, and to be female (never mind openly sexual as Mary, the prostitute, is). Despite the image of religious fidelity and simple honesty imposed by the idyllic mythology, there are drug-takers and dealers and street gangs; headbangers and punks are to be found in many places around the country. George, the ailing and aging con man, is perhaps the nearest of all to respectability, and representative of the old way of being poor in Ireland: a tenacious adherence to the maintenance of outward appearances (jacket, tie, waistcoat) in the face of crushing poverty. George is offered a place in a Corpo flat (public housing for the poor built by Dublin Corporation) and asks Jimmy to join him but, significantly, is refused. Jimmy prefers to go it alone; he actually likes something about his way of being and chooses to keep on in the old squat even though his eviction is imminent. In an odd sort of way, this seems to be a tribute to the tenacity of the Irish, and their ability to doggedly persist in the pursuit of elusive things. Cathal Black has shown us a character in Jimmy who, though an outcast from Irish society, exhibits those traits that have defined the Irish character over many centuries and have been celebrated in the country's history and mythology.

Returning to the theme of decay which permeates *Pigs,* it's well worth our while to look back at Cathal Black's previous film, *Our Boys.* Made in 1981 for about 17,000 punts and financed by Bord Scannan na hEireann (The Irish Film Board), Radio Telefis Eireann and the arts councils of both the Republic and Northern Ireland.

Although the look and feel of this film is very different from *Pigs,* the mark of the director is quite evident. *Our Boys* of the title are the young Irishmen educated in the schools run by the Christian Brothers. As with the later film, Black is again walking a fine line and thereby doing something of great subtlety and complexity. It would have been easy for him to make a paean to the Brothers or an outright condemnation of them and their methods of education and discipline, but he has instead painted a detailed, detached, and incisive picture and left us to judge.

The film is shot in monochrome and invested with a very strong documentary look and texture (again by Thaddeus O'Sullivan). This has been achieved by carefully interweaving the threads of three distinct elements: newsreel footage from the past, footage of actors playing the priests in a Christian Brothers school and a boy enrolled in the school and his family, and interview segments with grown men recounting their experiences as "our boys."

The scripted dramatic action revolves around Father Gilmartin (played by the fine actor Mick Lally). The film opens with footage of a Papal parade in College Green (in front of Trinity College, Dublin) from the 1950s, then cuts to scenes of the Brothers praying, having tea, lecturing, and beating the schoolboys. This is followed by a sequence of a man describing his being beaten as a child. Then follows a scene of the priests relaxing and talking, then one of the family of the boy who was shown being beaten, then an interview with a priest who is earnestly attempting to justify corporal punishment. We're shown more old newsreel shots (this time of a Papal visit to Ireland), followed with a scene of one of the Brothers lecturing about sin and punishment, then the boy's father complaining about his son being beaten. This is followed with an interview with another "old boy" describing the emotional effect of public humiliation, then by scenes of the Brothers negotiating the sale of the school and the attached land, then shots of schoolboys being stropped on the hands. The film then finishes with a sequence showing the senior priest ill in bed, then the younger priests packing, and the school empty and vandalized.

Black has made some really powerful images here. The intercutting of fictional dramatic footage with old news film and interviews with men who remembered the rough sort of corporal punishment meted out by the Christian Brothers make a potent and volatile mix. There is the risk in this approach that the line between fiction and fact becomes blurred, but Black achieves something quite different by carefully controlling the pace and placement of the constituent elements. What we see, finally, is a film which uses the devices of news, documentary, and fictionalized dramatic scenes to produce a statement about emotional impact and psychological effect rather than a simple laying out of factual information. As such, it's a much more powerful statement, and gives the film's audience a point-of-view/first-person vantage. It is neither a cold condemnation of the Christian Brothers and their methods nor an overly sentimental look at the old tradition of boys' education in Irish schools. What we see, instead, is a portrait of an archaic system of indoctrination which utilized self-doubt, corporal punishment, and militaristic discipline to discourage independent thought and unapproved behavior. It is ultimately a sort of death knell, a eulogy for a way of life and thought which has outlived its time and been discarded. There is little doubt that Black thinks things are better as they are than as they were; nonetheless, it is evident from Father Gilmartin's expression, as he takes a last look at the decaying old school building, that he is actually fearful of the world outside and aware that the tables have been turned and the rules changed. We *almost* feel a bit sad for him.

Joe Comerford: *Down the Corner*

Similar in feel, although predating *Our Boys* by three years, is Joe Comerford's first feature, *Down the Corner*. This too is invested with the strong feel of the docudrama, and though it's shot in color, the color is washed out and it gives an overall impression of drab greyness to the suburban Dublin streets and houses of Ballyfermot. Opening with an abrupt effect--the superimposition of a rubber stamp of the word "REDUNDANT" over a scene of a man working in a factory, the film proceeds to follow the effects of this on the man and his family (but most of all, his son). (For those not familiar with this application of the term, "redundant" means "laid-off" in Irish usage.)

The central event of the film is an act of theft: the son, Derek, and his friends plan the invasion of an orchard to steal apples, and in the process he cuts his leg and is taken to a hospital. There isn't much more to the plot, but that doesn't matter too much. This is an atmosphere piece, a kind of portrait which uses the simple incidents of a man losing his job, a group of boys committing an act of petty thievery, and the (possibly romanticized) recollections of an old granny about her experiences on the run with the old IRA in juxtaposition to one another to make its point. The concerns of each generation are markedly different from each other, and the lines of communication almost never connect.

The key to this film is its texture: the washed-out color of the present-tense footage and the black-and-white footage of the granny's recollections combine with the father's violence and the disrespect with which the children regard their elders to make a picture of working-class Dublin that is pretty bleak. (It will be echoed, albeit in a sentimentalized manner, in Roddy Doyle's *The Commitments* a dozen years later.) These pictures are set to the mournful music of the west of Ireland, a single male vocalist accompanied by a bodhran[4] drum. Add to this mix the peripheral character of the country doctor encountered in the city hospital, and in this comparison/contrast the rural agrarian culture and its mythology are seen to clash abruptly with the hard reality of modern urban cynicism. The mythology surrounding the agrarian stereotype is, of course, that which was officially sanctioned by the government in the period just prior to this, and it may be taken that a slap at that mythology was what Comerford had in mind.

Several years before, he had made a film called *Withdrawal,* which dealt with the plight of patients in a mental hospital dealing with their drug addictions. It was characteristic of Comerford that he would address an issue that the government had worked diligently to keep under wraps by confronting it full-front in a rather public way. As an art student, he had been involved in the student strike at the National College of Art and Design, and the tone had been set for a lifelong contentious relationship between himself and the powers that be. As a result, he has had difficulty getting his projects funded and, having made them, getting them shown (at least in his home country). He has also built himself a reputation for perfectionism and uncompromising adherence to his own artistic objectives.

Down the Corner caused some shock waves when it was made, and there were rumors of some contentiousness between Comerford and the members of the Ballyfermot community in which it was shot. Nonetheless, blunt instrument though it may have been, it proved to be prophetic in its way, and a rather poetic treatment of a difficult topic: the decay and abandonment of the Gaelic idyll among the people of Ireland's urban working classes. *Withdrawal* was prophetic in its anticipation that Dublin's drug problem would become one of the worst in Europe; *Down the Corner* was prophetic in that it anticipated the usefulness of Dublin's working-class neighborhoods as settings for the dramatic writing of people like Roddy Doyle and the Jim Sheridan/Shane Connaughton team, and helped to define the cinematic style with which it would be depicted in those later treatments. Until very recently, Joe Comerford's work had not been widely shown outside Ireland, and its showings within the country have been severely restricted, but the other filmmakers there are well aware of it and probably influenced by it. Although he often threatens to quit filmmaking, he continues to make more, and with increasingly greater character depth and polish. *High Boot Benny*, discussed in a later chapter, is his most recent and most finely crafted work.

Bob Quinn: *Budawanny* and *The Bishop's Story*

This is a good point from which to cast a look back to the more recent work of the man with whom we opened this chapter, Bob Quinn. Like Joe Comerford, he is an experimenter, and not afraid to return to a theme with a different treatment. Such is the case with his most recent effort, which is also one of his earlier films. (It is a trait these two filmmakers have in common--their work is difficult to categorize, and therein may lie the reason for some of the hostility and criticism shown to it on occasion.)

This film was originally called *Budawanny*, and was based upon a novel by Padraig Standun written in the Irish and entitled *Suil Le Breith*. (This was translated into English and unfortunately retitled *Lovers*, although the literal translation would be "The Eye of Judgment.") The story is centered around a priest in a small island community in the west, who takes in a pregnant woman as his housekeeper after her apparent suicide attempt. In a violent thunderstorm, she runs to his bed and from that a sexual relationship develops. Then her pregnancy develops, and the conflict around which the body of the story is built is the resultant dilemma, both for the lovers and for the community. In the event, most of the islanders are not terribly upset, and don't seem to mind that the priest and the housekeeper intend to live together with the child; the concern of the community is for the welfare of the priest, whom they have come to respect. One villager, the publican, disagrees and phones the bishop. A conflict ensues between priest and bishop, and is resolved when the girl leaves the island.

Once again, we are presented with a portrait of the Irish as other than we expect: the islanders' essential decency in their willingness to forgive the priest and the girl in spite of their transgression is consistent with the picture of the common folk given us in *It's Handy when People Don't Die* and *Anne Devlin*, and the adversarial nature of their relationship with the authority figure of the Church consistent with *Our Boys* and *The Kinkisha*. There is also a revealing exchange between the priest and bishop on the matter of the priest's behavior:

> Priest: "What would Christ do?"
> Bishop: "Leave Christ out of this."

Stylistically, the film is spare, restrained, and elegant to the point of being poetic. Quinn has set himself a difficult task by putting most of the dialogue in Gaelic, and adding English subtitles. In addition, he's telling the story in flashbacks, which are in monochrome intercut with color scenes of the bishop drafting a letter to the priest (presumably in the present). The effect, then, is to make the film reliant upon the visually dramatic footage and the musical score to set the mood and give the events their interpretation. This he does with great subtlety and beauty. The shots range from cozy to lively to stunningly dramatic largely without the aid of dialogue, relying on Quinn's eye and Roger Doyle's music. The overall impact is quite powerful and very personal, taking us into the lovers' relationship, setting the tone of the background society in which they are living, and finally making a statement that is both fatalistic and sad. By dwelling on the personal in this manner, he has (as Cathal Black did with *Pigs* and Pat Murphy with *Maeve*) managed to make a strong statement about society without climbing a soapbox to do so.

The recut version of *Budawanny* is titled *The Bishop's Story*, and Bob Quinn is adamant that the newer version suits him better. What he has done is to cast the love story further back in time, and to add in scenes of the priest--now a bishop himself--talking with another priest apparently being disciplined for indulging a fancy for altar boys. The flashback scenes are largely those of the previous film, although the Gaelic dialogue has been dubbed in, and the monochrome sequences seem to have a more documentary feel than they did before. The soundtrack has a more moody, eerie quality, and the whole thing has been framed much differently. The present-day dialogue scenes give Quinn the opportunity for more discourse on the nature of the Church, and particularly on the structure and politics which surround the now-incendiary issue of sexuality among the priesthood. In this version, the former-priest-now-bishop confesses to nonbelief and elaborates upon the inability of the Church to cope with someone such as himself: "When they can't fire you, they promote you." Finally, the

6. *Budawanny:* **Bob Quinn's adaptation of Padraig Standun's novel,** *Suil Le Breith,* **about love and sin among the islanders.** (Courtesy of the Irish Film Archive and Bob Quinn)

girl gets the opportunity to have her say by leaving a note for the priest
when she runs away: "It's my life too." Despite his non-belief and his
revisionist attitude toward celibacy, the priest is seen to regard the
girl's role as a subordinate one, and thus his character embodies a
double criticism of the Church as both a hypocritical organization in
the way it is administrated, and one which fails to address the needs
of women.

Many of the people referred to in this chapter have broken new
ground and shown exceptional artistic talent; their names will
reappear later, and nearly all continue to be involved in the indigenous
film community in Ireland and to make new films, however
sporadically. It is a particularly difficult task to fund and complete
this sort of work in an economic and political climate such as that in
which they are working; it stands as a tribute to the tenacity of these
filmmakers that they continue to produce and to maintain their
integrity of vision as they do so.   Comerford sums it up this way:

> I'm speaking to an Irish audience. For my survival I need to have the
> support of people outside Ireland. But the prime motivation is to
> make a film to be shown in Ireland.[5]

Notes

1. Rockett, Gibbons, Hill, *Cinema and Ireland*, p. 247.
2. Thomas Murphy, *A Crucial Week in the Life of a Grocer's
Assistant* (Dublin, Gallery Press, 1978): scene 11.
3. *Cinema and Ireland*, p. 243.
4. A bodhran is a handheld drum made of goatskin, an ancient
musical instrument still essential in the makeup of a traditional Irish
band.
5. Author's interview, June 1994.

CHAPTER SIX
NEIL JORDAN AND THE EMERGENT EIGHTIES

As a force to be reckoned with in the film world, Ireland is a bit like the actor who becomes an "overnight success" in New York or London after many years of hard work in the provinces. While the worldwide notoriety of *My Left Foot* was a Cinderella story for Jim Sheridan (who directed it) and Noel Pearson (who produced), it is fair to say that much groundwork was laid prior to that success by people like Neil Jordan and Pat O'Connor.

Neil Jordan and Pat O'Connor

Neil Jordan set out to be a writer of realist fiction. He has continued to write (*Sunrise with Sea Monster*[1] having recently been published), but he is most widely known in Ireland and abroad for the films he has directed. As was mentioned before, he was the scriptwriter for *Traveller* (directed by Joe Comerford), and it may well have been this experience which turned him from writing to directing. He was not particularly happy with the result of that film, which was, in the end, a statement of Comerford's view more than his.

Pat O'Connor came to film through RTE, where he had established himself as a solid director of television dramas (including *The Riordans*, the drama from which the still-running series *Glenroe* was a spin-off). He came to RTE after stints in London, Los Angeles, and Toronto, where he developed an interest in film and learned the rudiments of the craft. It was O'Connor who directed the RTE production of Jordan's *Night In Tunisia* and the RTE/BBC coproduction of *The Ballroom of Romance* (which is dealt with in chapter 3).

Jordan's opportunity to make a film himself came when John Boorman, who was at the time head of Ardmore Studios and shooting his own *Excalibur* there, invited him to make a documentary about the shooting of that Boorman feature. On the basis of that experience, and the lessons learned from several other projects in which he wrote scripts, Neil Jordan proceeded to shoot his first dramatic piece, *Angel,* in 1982.

Jordan: *Angel* and *The Crying Game*

Like *Traveller, Angel* is set in the North amid the fighting, yet distinctly divorced from it. As the protagonists in *Traveller* were outcasts from mainstream Irish society (and therefore also disinterested in the political conflict in the North), so the featured player in this film is a detached loner. The character is named Danny, and is an itinerant saxophone player traveling around to various resorts and country dance halls with a small, low-budget showband. (The protagonist's name is also the source of the unfortunate retitling of the film for the American market, *Danny Boy.*)

Danny (played by Stephen Rea, in his first association with Jordan) is a rather cryptic saxophonist who is unattached and seems to draw a lot of interest from the women who frequent the dance halls. In the opening of the film, we see him being followed by a rather plain young girl who never says anything, but stares at him with awe and admiration. He buys her a ticket to the dance, and we then see the full effect of the band in all its sequined regalia and cheap lighting effects. In the course of the night, Danny also becomes the focus of the attentions of a young newlywed (whose husband seems to have vanished) and we're led to believe that he has had some sort of romantic involvement with the band's singer too (played by Honor Heffernan). The film grows more and more surreal as the night wears on and people become more intoxicated, until it is positively dreamlike as Danny and the young girl go to a large concrete sewer pipe, sitting in a nearby field, for sex. It becomes apparent that she is deaf; Danny notices this fact just as a car pulls up and several men with weapons kill his band's manager (in a dispute over protection payments) before dynamiting the hall. They also kill the girl, who stands up and runs toward them at just the wrong moment.

The dream has turned to a nightmare, and it doesn't end until the last scene of the film. Danny encounters the police in the form of an Inspector Bloom (Ray MacAnally), who is quiet and deliberate, and utterly inscrutable. They will encounter each other several times, in each of which Bloom takes on a more omniscient character until he seems almost godlike at the end. In the meantime, Danny becomes fixated upon revenge. He tracks down one of the murderers by virtue of the man's club foot and, following him home, discovers an Armalite with which he surprises the man and kills him. Meantime, the band has reorganized, and they're touring again with a new manager. Danny and the singer become closer, developing a sexual relationship as Danny returns to his childhood home to live with his aunt Mae. Relentlessly, though his love relationship begins falling apart and his purpose is indistinct, Danny pursues the other killers.

Acting on information gained from a photo-identification session in the police station, he finds the second of the three men who murdered the girl. Following him to his cottage on the beach, Danny kills him with the same automatic weapon, which he now carries in an instrument case. Then, quite by accident, he meets the bride from the dance hall and, having slept with her, finds out where her husband is. (Remember that her husband was conspicuously absent from the dance hall just prior to the shooting.) Tracking the man down to his job in a forest, Danny slips into the man's car and shoots him, causing the car to drive off the road into a field. He leaves the car, with the man's girlfriend sobbing in the front seat, and stumbles toward a tent

on a beach, where his band is to play later on. There he discovers the
new manager making payments to another paramilitary-type, and
Danny shoots the man. Just at that moment, the singer comes in and
hears Danny explaining what he's been doing on his free time. She
screams at him, pushes him away. Danny stumbles out again, this
time acting like a fugitive.

He comes to a small farmhouse, where he surprises a woman in
the yard. There he discovers that she is a widow; at gunpoint he
demands that she give him a change of clothing and a haircut, which
she does. She makes a halfhearted attempt to stab him with a kitchen
knife, but only cuts his hand. Finally, he falls asleep and she pries the
gun from his hands--and shoots herself. Danny runs outside, starts a
van he finds there, and drives until he comes to a silver trailer
(caravan) where a carnival barker is touting fortune-telling sessions
with a boy who has mystical powers: the seventh son of a seventh son.
Danny speaks with the boy briefly, then faints on the floor. When he
wakes, another detective, Bloom's assistant Bonner, is there to take
Danny away. Instead of taking him to the police station, though, he
takes him to the burnt-out dance hall from the beginning of the film.
There, it becomes apparent that Bonner is one of the paramilitaries,
and Danny is to be executed. Just as he is about to be shot, though,
Bonner takes a hit from another gunman: Bloom, who has come in
behind Danny. Bloom has appeared, like an angel, from nowhere, and
the credits roll as ash and dust and papers blow around the place to the
thundering accompaniment of a helicopter.

As an adventure film--a detective story of a sort--*Angel* works
rather well. It keeps us wondering, it keeps taking unexpected turns,
and there are moments of tension which are quite well constructed. It
is as a dream piece that it works best, though. Jordan has done a fine
job of creating a surreal world in this film, one which seems to lack
tangible points of reference, and certainly leaves us with no idea as to
who are the good guys or the bad. The dance hall scenes and other
musical sequences are quite eerily staged and shot, especially one in
which the band plays a charity concert in a mental hospital. Equally,

the simple fact that the band is always traveling means that there are no points of reference for them. They seem to live onstage and in tacky dressing rooms or cheap hotel rooms which are unconnected; we rarely see them in transit from one to the other, and the film is structured in a way that follows Danny's stream of consciousness rather than a particular narrative line. The most strongly grounded locale is Aunt Mae's flat, but even there Jordan has introduced the surreal by making her a reader of tarot cards and foreteller of the future.

Throughout, Danny moves as if in a dream; he is distant from everyone and seems to relate strongly only to the deaf girl (who is herself an outcast). Although he sleeps with the singer on numerous occasions, he also quite easily does so with the young bride when he thinks it will get information from her. Despite this, he is seen to be a symbol for just behavior; Danny's actions are seemingly motivated by "an eye for an eye" and nothing more. It may be the strength of his feelings for the deaf girl, or it may be his outrage at seeing her so brutally killed, but he is a kind of avenging angel who sets out, without really being aware of it, to exact justice. On a larger scale, Jordan has done for us what we couldn't do ourselves--he has shown us what it is like to live in a situation in which the normal rules of society do not apply. One cannot trust the police: one officer, Bloom, is fair and evenhanded (perhaps because he's an outsider too, being Jewish) while the other is himself an outlaw. One cannot trust anyone who is not a personal acquaintance, since everyone has, or might have, a hidden affiliation which could make him your enemy. In such a climate of mistrust and suspicion, in which the normal preoccupation with personal objectives is supplanted with fear and paranoia, everyday life loses its quality of normality. What Jordan does with *Angel* is something he will do again and again: he shows us the personal impact of a violent society, and asks us what we as individuals would do in those circumstances. Is Danny good or evil? Is violence an acceptable response to violence? As he must do, Jordan leaves us with no answers; the ending is as unsettling as it is abrupt and inconclusive.

Nonetheless, a number of issues are raised in *Angel* and it may be the film's weakest aspect that too many are packed into the one piece. Aside from raising the question of the morality of violence, Jordan has also pulled in the issue of women's roles in violent conflict (largely as victims), the role of religion in the conflict in the North, mysticism/paganism, the mindlessness of political causes as they relate to the lives of individuals, and a strong note of nostalgia for the mundane but nonviolent past.

Aside from Aunt Mae (who also seems to be outside the society and its conflicts), all the women in this film are victims, directly or indirectly, of the violence that surrounds them. This is a theme which comes up again in Pat O'Connor's film *Cal*, and resurfaces with another face in Jordan's *The Crying Game*. As in Pat Murphy's *Maeve* and *Anne Devlin*, the conflict is portrayed as an essentially male one, in which the women are merely used by those who participate in the violence or are otherwise victimized. Even Danny, when he is overtaken by the need for violent revenge, is reduced to using women's trust in a callous way to gain his own ends. This costs him the affection of the singer, but by that time he is so numb as not to show any reaction. Thus the suicide of the farmer's widow seems, in the context of the killing which has surrounded it, almost a rational act: love is no longer possible, nurturing is no longer possible, life seems to have no meaning.

It is also significant that although we learn near the end that the paramilitaries who killed the deaf girl are Protestant, it is a fact of little consequence and one which is tossed out into our consciousness as a flippant offhand jibe at the last of the three killers by his Catholic girlfriend as they're going off to have sex in the forest. The details of the political situation are both assumed--as they might be when addressing an Irish audience already familiar with them--and (more significantly) unimportant. This could be happening anywhere; what is important is the individual caught in the situation: the unfair and brutal death of the deaf girl, the rage that ignites in Danny, and the subsequent effect it has on his thinking and life. In the process of interrogation, Danny discovers that Bloom is Jewish; to this he responds, "Protestant Jew or Catholic Jew?" The clear statement is that it doesn't matter: Danny's actions are more deeply rooted--more elemental--than those of his enemies, and their political/religious affiliations make no difference to him. Jordan is implying that, for all that his descent into violence taints Danny with the bloodlust of those against whom he is fighting, his quest may somehow be purer than theirs. His is a sort of modern-day martyrdom: he loses everything of value to himself in the process, but he does achieve a kind of justice in an inherently evil and unjust world.

What Jordan denies us in this instance--the thing that is denied us by many contemporary Irish filmmakers--is a conventional resolution. He is content with (in fact, intent upon) an ending that wraps up nothing and leaves us puzzling about what happened and why. It is essential to his task, if he is to make us deal with the events and issues at hand in a personal way, that he refrain absolutely from mounting the soapbox and turning polemical. This he does with rigorous faith; at no point are we certain that the paramilitary types whom Danny is pursuing are wholly bad or that Danny, in his quest for revenge, is wholly good. All we are certain is that anyone who wades into a sewer will be covered with muck; all that is clearly stated is that violence begets violence and everyone is ultimately the poorer because of that.

Jordan took some harsh criticism from the Irish press for this stand. He clearly failed to articulate a position of political advocacy on either side of the divide that exists in the North, refusing as he did to frame the conflict in any sort of political terms. This was no accident, and it is clear that his refusal to do so was genuinely felt and consistently adhered to, as is evident in the reworking of the themes addressed in *Angel*: his most successful film, *The Crying Game*.

Although the film was made nearly ten years later, the idea for *The Crying Game* began with a story written by Jordan in 1983, the year after *Angel* was made. Having made one kind of statement (albeit a non-polemical one) about the violence in the North, he set out to pursue that with something stronger and a bit more focused when he revisited the subject:

> . . . in this film, *The Crying Game,* I did want to make something that came out of the nationalist point of view. I wanted the Stephen Rea character to have a certain coherent set of beliefs. I didn't want him to be a psychopath. I didn't want him to be someone who was bruised by circumstances or whatever.   I just wanted him to be someone who had a pretty good perspective himself.[2]

This time, the protagonist is clearly and consciously involved in the conflict, on the side of the nationalist paramilitaries, the Provisional IRA (Provos). Once again, as in *Night in Tunisia,* Jordan is drawn to the seaside resort as a backdrop for his opening scene, in this case to draw a sharp contrast between the image of civilian holidaymakers in a state of relaxed enjoyment and the underlying reality of Northern Irish life. From the opening sequence, the film begins its process of peeling away the layers of this onion, showing us that absolutely nothing is what it seems to be. As a device for the personalized treatment of its subject, Jordan has found in this a better one than the dreamlike unreality of *Angel.* Ultimately, Danny's dream is *his* and not ours; by showing us scenes with realistic clarity and then turning them inside out, *The Crying Game* adds a kind of sparring gamesmanship to the dialogue between director and audience which draws us deeper into it and thereby makes its impact all the more personal and direct.

The Miranda Richardson character, Jude, is really neither the blonde nor the civilian she appears to be in the opening scenes, and her date with the British soldier Jody (played by Forest Whitaker) nothing to do with affection or even sexual interest, but a means of entrapment and ultimately death. It is not too much of a surprise that the Stephen Rea character, Fergus, turns out to be softer than his compatriots and shows some sympathy to the soldier. What is a surprise is the way in which the soldier is killed (being run down accidentally by one of his own army's Saracen tanks) and the timing of the British assault on the Provo hideout, which leaves Fergus a means of escape both from the personally repellent task of killing the soldier Jody (whom he has befriended) and from his identity as a soldier in the IRA and concomitant role in the fighting.   This did, as we shall see, refer back to the title character's dilemma in Pat O'Connor's film *Cal* of a decade earlier.

Thus the film is begun as an adventure story firmly grounded in the facts of the conflict in Northern Ireland, and until well into its travels, a seemingly straightforward preamble to the story of Fergus's flight to a new and more palatable way of life in England. In the event, it turns out to be something quite different, but the first part of the film, taken separately, makes several strong statements.

It is worth noting here the long association between Neil Jordan and the fine actor Stephen Rea; certainly a fruitful artistic joint venture, but much more than that. Jordan has written three roles with Rea in mind in which his character is a fairly unexceptional Irish man faced with a very difficult moral choice. We have seen this in the role of Danny in *Angel,* we see it in Fergus here, and will see it again in the character of Ned Broy in *Michael Collins:* the low-level agent of the Dublin police who chooses to betray his British masters and serve as an inside spy for Collins and the old IRA. This device, of an Irish Everyman faced with the need to choose between his politics and his ethics, is a favorite device of Jordan's when he asks us to consider the political/moral dilemmas of recent Irish history, and is made all the more poignant by the fact that the same actor has played this role in each of the films in which it was used.

Firstly, the Rea character, like Danny in *Angel,* is an essentially nonviolent person who is drawn into the conflict. In *The Crying Game,* however, he is drawn in for political or social reasons (remember the theme of *High Boot Benny*) rather than anything so pure as rage. He is in this instance a reluctant soldier, as his discussions with Jody (the British soldier) reveal: Fergus merely recites the Provos' rhetoric without much passion or conviction. We are thus prepared to think of him as someone with his own ideas; a soldier of the IRA who nonetheless questions what they are doing and has some strong reservations about shooting a handcuffed prisoner.

He is, as was Danny, functioning from a higher moral ground than the other paramilitaries. He is also more honest and naive than his Provo comrades, qualities which perhaps order his priorities differently from theirs.

Secondly, the choice of a black soldier makes a strong statement about the political use made of the conflict in the North by successive British governments. It is apparently no accident that a member of an oppressed minority in English society is sent to fight members of another such minority in Northern Ireland. It is a sign of Fergus's greater intellectual capacity (as compared with the other Provos) that he can see the essential common ground between himself and Jody: both are victims of the conflict, and both seem to suspect that they may be disposable pawns in someone else's game. Thus it is a political statement that Jody is killed by his own army rather than the Provos: as a poor black Englishman, he is regarded by his own country's leaders as disposable, and his death is both brutally violent and relatively inconsequential. This is an aspect of the Northern Irish conflict that is rarely dealt with; nevertheless, the existence of wartime conditions there has given politicians in Britain both a reason to maintain a vestige of the old imperial army (a place to put the unemployed young men from London and the industrial cities of the North of England who might otherwise engage in civil unrest) and a means of stirring up the kind of blind patriotism and political conservatism that keeps them in power and, to some extent, diverts public attention from the serious economic troubles which plague Britain.

Having escaped miraculously from the holocaust rained upon the Provo hideout by the British troops, Danny makes his way surreptitiously to London, where he finds work as a casual laborer on a construction site. He has changed his name, assumed a new identity, and severed all his links with the North of Ireland and the Troubles, except one: he's kept Jody's wallet, given him along with the demand that he look up Jody's girlfriend (whose name is Dil) in London.

After a time, he does that. He finds her at her place of employment--a hairdressing salon--and meets her in a local pub for a drink. A relationship develops (along the lines of that which we shall see is the central device of *Cal*), and we begin to see the effect that the events of the first part are having on Fergus. By his actions he seems to be filling in for Jody, and the dreams he has in which Jody appears seem to confirm the rightness of this action. Their relationship seems to be solidly cemented when Fergus chases away Dil's abusive boyfriend, and the story seems to be headed in the direction of the revelation to her of Fergus's role in Jody's death and the consequences that may have.

Then comes the truly shocking revelation--that Dil is not a woman, but a quite convincing transvestite. Stunned, Fergus runs away, but Dil pursues him and they reach some sort of uneasy friendship in which Fergus seems to be reluctant and fascinated at the same time. In Fergus's dream, Jody is now grinning; even in death, he's had the last laugh. Then, from nowhere, Jude reappears to reenlist Fergus in the cause. Unlike the women in *Angel*, Jude is the quintessential ice-cold soulless killer, and she threatens a painful punishment for Dil if Fergus declines to help the Provos assassinate a British judge. Now Fergus's head is really swimming: he'd looked for some consolation for his guilt about Jody's death in Dil only to be knocked askew by Dil's real identity, and now his past, from which he thought he'd escaped, has caught up with him in all its ruthless violence.

In an attempt to save Dil, he dresses her (him) in a man's clothing and relocates her to a hotel. Then Fergus sets out to prepare for the assassination. Dil, however, follows him and they go to her flat, where Fergus confesses to a very drunk Dil that he had a hand in Jody's death. The assassination is to happen the following morning, but Fergus wakes to find that Dil has tied him to the bed and is pointing his gun at him. She threatens him with it, but can't shoot him. Meanwhile, Jude and Maguire (the Provo leader) are attempting the assassination without Fergus. It goes badly awry, and Maguire is killed. Jude escapes and turns up at Dil's flat with execution in mind, but (in another turnabout) Dil very slowly kills her with Fergus's gun, after deducing that it was Jude who laid the trap for Jody.

The film ends with Fergus in jail and Dil, again dressed as a woman, coming to visit him. The last thing we hear is Fergus reciting to Dil a fable about a frog and a scorpion which Jody had told to Fergus while he was Fergus's prisoner. In the fable, the frog gives the scorpion a lift across a river, but the scorpion stings the frog halfway across and they both drown. With his last breath the frog asks why and the scorpion explains, "It's in my nature."

Ten years on, the statement made in this film is much stronger and more sharply focused than it was in *Angel*. There was, once again, harsh criticism in Ireland. Apart from those who opposed the characterization of the Provos as mindless killers (remember it was Protestant paramilitaries in the previous film), there was criticism over the character of Jude from the Irish feminist movement. In the United States, the transvestism (of the Dil character) became the point of discussion for many cinemagoers and critics, to the exclusion of the political statement. Jordan, however, had something else in mind when he wrote the script:

> I wrote her [Jude] quite consciously as a monster, a monstrous part, because all the men who survive make female choices and the woman makes male choices. It's very consciously done. Well, Stephen [Fergus] only survives by becoming a woman, in a way. I mean, only survives by not becoming a woman but by taking on what you would think of as feminine virtues, you know, more understanding, compassionate. The corollary of that is that the woman would become more like a man. I don't understand what's offensive about it.[3]

What was offensive about that portrayal of the situation is less important than whom it ought to offend. Clearly, the broadside here is again directed at those who trade in violence. From the outset, Fergus is established as the sympathetic character: he is likable in his demeanor, thoughtful, and concerned about the ethics of his comrades and the morality of their actions (and his). He likes Jody and treats him with respect (while the others, including Jude, pistol-whip him while he is bound and hooded). The presence of Fergus in the protagonist role prods us to ask whether we might not do the same in the same situation. He is essentially a decent person of no particularly strong commitments--rather like most of us. He is clearly the hero of the piece; we want him to escape to London safely and we hope all along that he might allow Jody to escape. Thus, when he encounters Dil and their relationship begins to blossom, it looks as though it may turn into a fairly hopeful love story, and we wish them both well in that regard.

The dual rude awakenings--sexual and political--which shock Fergus out of his reverie come as equally powerful shocks to the audience. He's stuck in a particularly thorny dilemma: he must rely on what is (for him) a sexually distasteful alliance or forsake his essentially nonviolent self and rejoin the Provos, who seem only to represent violent death. The choice he makes--given the stamp of approval by its upbeat tone in the final scene--is clearly the one of life over death, even if that means a long prison term and the acceptance of love from another male. This is a slap at the paramilitary segment of Northern Irish society in a much clearer and more direct way than in *Angel*. Unlike Danny, Fergus thinks things through: he has taken sides on the political issue, and clearly chooses to renege on that choice, even if it threatens his sexual identity.

Where the killers in *Angel* were depicted as rather nonspecific representatives of an insidious undercurrent of society, the ones in *The Crying Game* are quite sharply drawn and evil in very specific, intentional ways. The evil act of *Angel* is the incidental, almost accidental, murder of an innocent bystander--someone who is utterly outside the conflict. In the second film, all the principals except Dil are part of the conflict, and yet the Provos are still presented as the purveyors of evil and Dil's prolonged and bloody execution of Jude is plainly the triumph of good.

Sexual identity is a sensitive issue in any culture, and an especially sensitive one in Ireland, where the feminist and gay movements are relatively younger than in England and the United States. The encoding of women's roles in society into law and the influence of the Church on the hot topics of abortion and divorce, as well as the uncertain status of gays and Lesbians in Irish society virtually guaranteed Jordan some vigorous debate over this film. The linking of sexual and political issues, especially the characterization of paramilitary violence as both evil and inherently masculine, would be certain to stimulate some strong reactions among the Irish audience.

In essence, though, he's not making any new or earth-shattering analogy: *Maeve* made the same statement, but in a more didactic, less sensational manner. From the idea that violence is essentially a male pastime, Neil Jordan has extrapolated the notion that violence is a product of the masculine side of an individual persona, and that participation in it must render the woman (Jude) more masculine than the men whom she despises, Fergus and Dil. In this approach he remains consistent throughout the film and, if not killing two birds with the one stone, certainly giving both nests a thorough stirring up.

Pat O'Connor: *Cal*

Thematically quite similar, and dating from the same period as *Angel* and the original story that became *The Crying Game,* is Pat O'Connor's film of Bernard McLaverty's novel *Cal.* This film belongs alongside *Angel*, since it shows the Troubles in the same stage of development and is thus not informed by hindsight as were *The Crying Game* and *In the Name of the Father* (the 1993 film by Jim Sheridan and Terry George).

It foreshadows *The Crying Game* in its treatment of sexual and political issues in the same relationship, and reflects its precursor *Angel* in its undertone of desperation and hopelessness. The story line is also somewhat less complex.   Cal (played by John Lynch) is presented as a young man from a working-class Catholic family living in a predominantly Protestant housing estate in the North, apparently in Derry. (Interestingly, the entire film was shot in the Republic--in counties Meath and Kildare--due to the instability of the Northern situation.) His father is a butcher, and the scene in which we first see the father is set in an abattoir, bloody animal carcasses hanging from meat hooks and his clothing and hands stained with blood. Apparently unknown to his father, Cal (although a quiet, reserved sort) is involved with the Provos. Like Fergus, he is without strong convictions on the political issues; he just knows that his prospects are severely limited in Northern Irish society because he comes from a Catholic family, and he is reminded of the unfairness of that on a daily basis.

The Provos in this film, unlike those of Jordan's *Angel*, are depicted with rather more depth. Skeffington, the leader of Cal's unit, is played by John Kavanagh as an obsessive second or third generation republican, and survivor of 1972's Bloody Sunday massacre in Derry, who idolizes his senile old father and can be relied upon to pontificate at length on the history of the conflict. He also is ruthlessly violent, but we see here a sense of the rationale behind the cause, however unsympathetic that presentation may be. The critical action of the film, which is reinforced later in Cal's flashbacks, is the assassination of an officer of the Royal Ulster Constabulary (the Northern Ireland police force, largely made up of Protestants). Cal was the driver for that hit, and the opening sequence of the film is a series of point-of-view shots of that event. We will be shown the view through that rainy windscreen of the drive up to the officer's house many times, as Cal relives it over and over again.

What happens to Cal, as a result of his participation in the killing of the policeman, is a sort of morbid fascination with Marcella (played by Helen Mirren), the woman whom his actions have widowed. She's a librarian, and Cal finds himself following her and arranging to meet her "accidentally" on the street. He discovers that, though she was married to a Protestant, she too is Catholic. Meanwhile, we are shown scenes of life with Cal and his father: parades of Orangemen (militant Protestants) in the street outside their house, nights of fitful sleep between street fights and car burnings, and finally threats from their Protestant neighbors to "burn them out."

By a combination of dumb luck and connivance, Cal contrives to be hired to work for a Mr. Dunlop (Ray MacAnally), the supervisor on the farm where Marcella lives with her dead husband's parents. As he spends time there, he comes to know the family better and to learn, to his pain, the effect his actions have had. He sees the old father-in-law crippled by an errant gunshot and Marcella's little girl left fatherless. Then the inevitable happens: a few days after being badly beaten by Protestant thugs in an alleyway, Cal returns home to find the house on fire, and his father sitting on the curb.

He and his father go to stay with an uncle, and Cal gets an idea: he will surreptitiously move into an old abandoned cottage on the farm, and thereby escape both the violence of the city and the Provos, whom he has told he wants out. Thus begins the second phase of this film--like *Maeve* and *The Crying Game,* we are shown a person who chooses not to continue association with the violence and is given the opportunity to begin again and sever those ties. The old lady (Marcella's mother-in-law) sees Cal's light in the cottage window, however, and the RUC come and brutally roust him from sleep. Marcella identifies him as an employee before the police can take him away, and the old woman tends his head wound and invites him to become a legal tenant in the cottage. Cal is a bit dumbfounded by the unexpected kindness of this gesture and offers to pay rent, but she refuses.

Time passes, and Cal and Marcella become friendly; she even confides to him her desperation with her situation and her desire to leave the farm and her in-laws. Still, his new life is comparatively idyllic and peaceful, and Cal only leaves the farm once, to visit his dad. What he finds is that his father has gone into a state of catatonic depression, sitting for hours and days in a chair doing nothing. Cal also finds that the Provos have been looking for him.

Back at the farm, he and Marcella are growing more intimate, and after a false start and a reconciliation, they become lovers. The old man has become very ill, and the old woman has gone with him to the hospital, so the two lovers have the farm and house to themselves, and they make liberal use of this opportunity to further their courtship.

As the old man is carried out on a stretcher, bundled into the ambulance and taken away, Cal pauses for a moment to watch as yet another vehicle drives away down the lane. The focal point of his flashbacks, the lane is at this moment both a reminder of past actions (and their ugly consequences) and a foreshadowing of Cal's imminent departure in another sort of van.

When the others have all left, Cal goes back into the house to lock up. Realizing that he's alone, he begins to wander around the place, predictably finding himself in Marcella's room. While there, he helps himself to various artifacts from her life: schoolbooks, photographs, mementos of her past. There is none of the sense of violation to this that there was in the similar scene in Kieran Hickey's *Exposure*. Rather, we see here the depth of Cal's infatuation with Marcella. He touches her things with tenderness; he is clearly trying to get closer to her, to get into her mind and life, and it is no surprise when he finally dozes off in her bed, his head buried in her pillow.

But there is more to this sequence. In addition to Marcella's privacy, Cal is also becoming privy to the personal lives of a wealthy Protestant family, a lifestyle starkly contrasted to his own rougher working-class Catholic world. Here he finally crosses over into the inner sanctum of his traditional enemies. It is a brief but important journey into hitherto unknown and mysterious territory, and as such is illustrative of the gulf between factions in the two societies of the North. As a poor urban Catholic, Cal would never have expected to see the inside of a Protestant country house, and so it is with awe and on tiptoe that he ventures from one room to another. But venture he does, and here he crosses the line, embracing in some way his historical foe--from this point there is no turning back, and for him the die is now cast and we know that he will surrender to it.

The scene in which he and Marcella first make love is rapidly intercut with shots from the murder of Marcella's husband, and we hear him calling out her name as he is dying while Cal mouths it too in the moment of climax. The contrast between love and violence is starkly drawn, and we also sense that Cal is in some way trying to fill the gap he's helped to create in Marcella's life.

Cal finally makes the fatal error: he goes into the city again at Christmas to buy presents. While buying a doll in a toy shop, he meets Crilly, the man who shot Marcella's husband. Crilly has just planted a bomb in the shop, and he takes Cal off to meet Skeffington. En route, Cal learns that his dad has been taken to a mental asylum, and that Crilly has carried out a kneecapping (described in detail, in which the victim's kneecaps are split by shooting them, rendering the person crippled but still alive to be seen as an example by others).

They're picked up by a car with Skeffington in the back seat, on the way out of the city. Cal is interrogated about his activities and he reiterates his desire to get out of the organization. This gives rise to the line which states a central point of the film: "The price of getting out is staying in." It seems certain that Cal is himself destined for a kneecapping, until the car is stopped at a British Army roadblock. The driver panics, the car runs off the road, and in the ensuing chaos Cal escapes. Skeffington is killed, but Crilly and the driver survive, Crilly shouting after Cal, "I'll get you for this." Cal runs to the only place he feels safe--the farm. He arrives at dawn and wakes Marcella to tell her that he's in trouble and can't tell her why, but that he would die for her. The RUC arrive shortly after and find him huddled in the cottage. After punching him a few times, they drag him to the police van and take him away. As the music wells up, we are shown the reverse of the opening shot: Cal's point of view from the back of the police van as he retreats down the drive away from the house, Marcella's image receding, alone, in the distance.

O'Connor took some criticism as well for *Cal* (any film dealing with the Northern conflict can be guaranteed to generate controversy on both sides of the border). As with *Angel*, there was complaint about the lack of a political stance; once again, an Irish filmmaker had addressed the problem in the context of a personal crisis of conscience rather than using the dramatic medium to make a political statement.

The refusal to make film a medium for the polemic has been a point of contention for several indigenous Irish filmmakers, and is related to the argument over censorship. When film was not being looked upon as a means of generating employment for Irish workers, it was viewed as a propaganda tool, either for those in control to use to their benefit or for others, whose point of view may have been regarded as distasteful, to use against them.   It may thus be a statement of a kind when filmmakers refuse to fit their work into either the commercial or the polemical mold: that is when they make a stand for art cinema, and that is what many Irish directors and writers have done.

Cal was, however, to be Pat O'Connor's last film on an Irish theme until 1995's *Circle of Friends*--a film with only tenuous Irish connections.   He has effectively transferred his base of operations to the United States and not addressed the Irish condition or the Irish audience since.   Neil Jordan, on the other hand, has kept returning to Irish themes at the same time as he has made films in Los Angeles and London.   His films have not generally been well received in his own country, but Jordan still regards himself as an Irish voice and endeavors to speak to the Irish condition.

Later Jordan Films: *The Company of Wolves* through *The Miracle*

Angel was followed by *The Company of Wolves* and *Mona Lisa,* both made in England, and neither concerned directly with Irish themes.   Nonetheless, they are both deeply stamped with the mark of their maker, and with a viewpoint that has much to do with his Irish background.   In both films, there is the underlying sense of surrealism which Jordan likes; *Wolves* is a fairy tale, and *Mona Lisa* takes place in the seedy underworld of London's West End pornography industry.

Being Irish often seems to entail taking the side of the underdog or going out of one's way to see another side of an issue.   This comes, in all likelihood, from an historical position on the wrong side of the bargain and a history of misrepresentation by one's oppressors.   Thus it is a characteristically Irish approach to the accepted fairy tale of

Little Red Riding Hood in which the viewpoint of the wolf is given sympathetic treatment. It is also characteristic of Neil Jordan that the underlying sexuality of the fairy tale is brought to the forefront and used as the device whereby the tale is turned on its head. In this version of the old story, the wolf presents a seductively sexual argument to the young girl Rosaleen, and she opts for it. In a way, the wolves are made to seem the more honest ones as regards our sexual nature, and the humans to seem the more hypocritical. Rosaleen strays from the path (both literally and figuratively): we're given a pretty clear picture of the qualities which she finds attractive in that, and no reason to believe that she suffers for it.

The Company of Wolves was a collaboration with the writer Angela Carter, and was followed by a collaboration with David Leland in *Mona Lisa.* In this film, Bob Hoskins plays an East End London lowlife whose life we enter as he's being released from prison. He returns to his old haunts and moves into a trailer (caravan) inside an old warehouse with his friend Thomas (played by Robbie Coltrane). Thomas is in the business of selling odd things (plastic statues of saints, plastic food, etc.), and the two of them describe everything that happens in the third person--in terms of the plot of an imagined detective novel. It's a clever device, and one which serves to narrate portions of the film without stepping out of the context of the plot itself. Hoskins's character is put to work by one of his old bosses, a pimp and operator of sex clubs (played by Michael Caine) as a driver for an upmarket black call girl (played by Cathy Tyson). He has an underlying dislike for her, tinged with racism, but is gradually won around to liking and respecting her, even to assisting her in a search for a younger prostitute whom she'd befriended earlier.

The film ends in confusion and violence. Hoskins and Tyson and the girl wind up in a hotel on the seashore (a favorite Jordan locale), and he discovers that the two are Lesbian lovers and that his vague romantic imaginings as regards Tyson are merely ludicrous. The Michael Caine character intrudes and Tyson kills him in a tearful rage, slowly and bloodily, exactly as Dil would later kill Jude in *The Crying Game.* Also like the later film, this one ends on a decidedly upbeat note, Hoskins and his estranged daughter taking the first steps to rebuilding their relationship.

With this film, we have the seeds of the themes to be reworked in the second part of *The Crying Game:* an outsider, attempting to start life anew in a world of violence, being confronted with conflicting ideas about race and gender and coming to terms with those things in a way that permits him to carry on. Like Fergus, Bob Hoskins's character is a reluctant hero; his situation forces him to dig deeper within himself and we find that he has some substantive redeeming qualities that permit him to summon up enough strength to deal with his circumstances. Also, as with most of Jordan's films, these two are intensely personal.

It has seemed to be his misfortune that Neil Jordan would be misunderstood and miscast by the filmmaking community in Los Angeles, though this shouldn't come as a great shock given the cultural differences between Ireland and California and the commercialism which drives the L.A. studios. The two early films Jordan shot in Hollywood stand in testament to the very different outlook on the art of filmmaking held by those in Ireland. The first of these was the remake of *We're No Angels,* adapted from the original by David Mamet. This film was a box-office failure, and widely ignored. The other, perhaps unfortunately, got some attention. This was a slapstick farce called *High Spirits,* which featured Peter O'Toole, Daryl Hannah, and Steve Guttenberg. It poked fun at Americans' stereotypes of Irish life, at the relish with which the Irish (both living and dead) would part the American tourists from their money, and the lengths to which they would go to do it. It was shot entirely in Los Angeles, except for some exteriors, and was finally a rather thin effort which failed to amuse either Irish or American audiences, and succeeded in generating some hostility from both.

If *The Crying Game* was a return visit to the themes of *Angel* and *Mona Lisa,* Jordan's 1991 project, *The Miracle,* represents a reworking of *Night In Tunisia.* This was an early short story (from the collection of the same name originally published in 1976) written by Jordan and directed for RTE television by Pat O'Connor. In *The Miracle* he revisits the fundamental theme and situation of this earlier piece and, as with *Angel,* updates it and makes the characters more complex and more sharply etched.

The Miracle is set in Bray, County Wicklow, and is a return to situations and metaphors Jordan has used in many of his films: the seaside resort, sexual coming-of-age, and the saxophone as a metaphor for a young man's struggle to reconcile himself with his father and the past. (Bray, you may remember, is also the location of the National Film Studios--ironically, an icon for some people of past governments' failure to deal adequately with the indigenous film movement.)

Like its precursor, this film follows the events in the life of a young man who lives in a typical seaside Irish town, replete with a white-sand beach, tacky carnival rides, and Victorian guest houses and hotels. Bray is similar to many other such towns in its geography: beside the strand is a very high grassy bluff, Bray Head, which rises abruptly from the sea and makes both a dominating land feature and a great vantage point. The town is connected to Dublin to the north by an electrified rail line, the DART (for Dublin Area Rapid Transit), which permits access to and from Dublin in thirty minutes or so.

This young man, Jimmy (Niall Byrne), is the son of a saxophone player (Donal McCann) who works in a local dance hall at night and usually comes home drunk and depressed, presumably something to do with the fact that Jimmy's mother has long since died. Jimmy spends his time with his friend Rose (Lorraine Pilkington) walking around the town and the strand watching people and hanging out in the fish-and-chip shops. The film opens with the pair of them watching an old couple and imagining the plot of a novel, in which they decide that the old man is trying to work up the courage to speak to the old woman and the old woman is waiting for him to do so. Walking further, they see an attractive younger woman, probably in her thirties, sunning herself on the bluff and reading. Intrigued, they decide she must be a Frenchwoman on the run from a mysterious past. When the woman goes swimming, they sneak up and look through her things for a clue to her identity; instead, she sees them and chases them off.

The following day they see her again, and make their apologies to her. They see her in Bray several times more, and Jimmy becomes fascinated with her, to the point of obsession. He decides he wants to make love with her, and Rose is enlisted to help. Throughout, Rose acts as Jimmy's confidante and advisor, a relationship which reprises the Hoskins/Coltrane friendship from *Mona Lisa,* even down to the affectation of speaking about themselves in the third person as if writing the plot for a novel.   Rose decides that she too wants a romantic involvement this summer, and sets her eye on a rude elephant trainer at the circus, which has just come to town. She then enlists Jimmy's assistance in her quest, and the two friends set about helping each other achieve their goals.

Jimmy, however, is truly obsessed, and we find him going off on his own, following the woman--who turns out to be an American actress--to the Olympia Theatre in Dublin where she's performing. Meantime, Jimmy has joined his father's band at the dance hall, and then quit because he found it dull. He is hired to play for the circus band, which gives him and Rose an excuse to be on the circus grounds any time they like, an opportunity she uses to interact with the elephant handler.

Coming home drunk, Jimmy's father finds a poster from the play in which the actress is performing (it's *Destry Rides Again*) and argues with Jimmy in a muddled fashion, telling him he's to stop seeing her. This, of course, has the opposite effect: Jimmy continues to go into the city to see her performances and to meet her backstage. She, however, seems edgy and always rebuffs his advances. Eventually, Jimmy sees his father backstage talking with the actress, and deduces that he has warned her to stay away. This causes a furious row at home, in which Jimmy and his father come to blows, apparently for the first time in their lives. The effect is that Jimmy sulks wordlessly for days, only talking to Rose, whom we discover swimming with him the next day. It begins to storm, so they grab their clothing and duck into a church for shelter. Giggling, Rose lights a candle and prays for Jimmy to get laid. Jimmy, looking at the plaster statue of Christ, says, "He doesn't say much, does he?" Jimmy's father apologizes for hitting him, but

Jimmy remains silent. That night, he again sees his father talking to the actress in the theater. By now we know that the actress is really Jimmy's mother, but Jimmy, still in the dark, pursues her again. In her hotel lobby, they have a shouting argument, and he storms off home.

The following evening, he and Rose go to the theater and again they see his father there with the actress. Still, they go backstage, and she promises that she'll come to the circus to see him play. On the train home, Rose admits to being jealous of her and we see (although Jimmy still doesn't) that Rose has been in love with him all along. The actress, however, doesn't come to the circus as she had promised to do. Home again, Jimmy makes up with his father, and agrees to rejoin the dance band. Unexpectedly, the actress shows up at the dance hall and then runs out; Jimmy runs out too, after shouting obscenities at his father and throwing down his instrument. Outside, he catches her and invites her around to the house. They have a few drinks, and he begins to make sexual advances, which she rebuffs again. Flustered, she runs out, leaving her handbag behind. Jimmy opens it and finds pictures of younger versions of herself and his father. Then his father comes home and, finally, tells him the truth about his mother.

The next morning, the phone rings as Jimmy's dad sleeps off his daily hangover. Jimmy answers it--it is the actress--and hangs up on her. He goes out walking and sees the old man and old woman again; this time he introduces them to each other and leaves them talking together. He meets Rose at the circus, and on her instructions, kisses her passionately in front of the elephant handler--presumably to make him jealous. Later that evening, the actress comes to the house asking if she can get her handbag. Jimmy lets her in and leaves; we then see that he's returned the photos so she won't know that he knows who she is. She follows him to the bluff, where he pretends to try to seduce her, thereby forcing her to tell him the truth. As they talk, we cut away to scenes of his father getting drunk and talking things through with the bandleader, and of Rose lying disinterestedly under the groaning and panting animal handler, her hand on his ring of keys.

Morning comes: the actress falls asleep on the grass and Jimmy leaves her there; Jimmy's dad sits on the railway tracks watching the approaching train, then slowly moves out of harm's way; Jimmy goes back to the church to pray for a sign from God.

Jimmy eventually falls asleep; there has been no sign, no miracle. When he wakes, though, there's an elephant in the church. He takes it by the trunk to lead it back to the circus, and finds Rose, with the keys to the animal cages in her hand. Having released all the animals, she throws the keys into the ocean below, and the two of them walk away from the camera talking about the plot for their love story.

Though much less violent or shocking than *The Crying Game*, this film cleverly incorporates some contentious imagery within the context of a rather sweet and quirky love story. Of course, there is the Oedipal theme of a son lusting after his mother; in the classical play and in this film, he is exonerated somewhat in our eyes by his own ignorance of their relationship, though the film's outcome is far from tragic. In a sense, that conflict is treated as an incidental detail--a reason why the actress is unattainable for Jimmy and also a means of humanizing her.

As with many coming-of-age stories, this treats the process as both one of losing virginity and of losing idealism and the sense of mystery. In the beginning, Jimmy is fascinated by the woman's exotic beauty and apparent mystique--she is presumably not Irish, as he surmises by her elegance of carriage and her expensive clothing. Jimmy quite plainly states this the first time he converses with her, asking her why an elegant lady such as she would come to Ireland, except to hide from someone. (The irony there, though both are unaware of it at that moment, is that she's come to find *him*.) In the course of the film, he discovers that she is no goddess; she's sexually inaccessible to him not because she's foreign and exotic but because she's far closer to him than he could have imagined: because his father has already been her lover, and she's his mother.

Like many modern Irish youth, Rose and Jimmy have lost faith in their parents' beliefs and their parents' aspirations. In one scene, they are on a golf course near the railway line, where Rose's father (played in a cameo appearance by the screenwriter and novelist Shane Connaughton) is playing; as he is eyeing up a stroke, Rose jumps in front of an oncoming train and shouts for help, but he doesn't turn around. The lack of communication between these young people and their parents is plainly demonstrated, yet finally, Jimmy and his father come to a very close understanding in which the theme of the film is embodied.

The film is titled *The Miracle,* but there is no miracle. After all the turmoil and disturbing revelations, Jimmy winds up in the church praying for a sign. Jordan gives us a succession of increasingly tighter close-ups of the faces of the plaster saints and Christ, but nothing happens. Finally, Jimmy wakes up to find the elephant--a sign from Rose, not a sign from God. That is the miracle, of course: it's quite like the miracle of discovery in *It's A Wonderful Life* but without the artifice of divine intervention. Jimmy finds, in the end, that the mysterious object he desires is neither mysterious nor desirable; his country, which he had denigrated, now seems bearable and his friend Rose, whom he'd overlooked as a woman, seems likely to become his lover as well. Finally, the "miracle" was simply the realization that he didn't need a miracle; that he already had what he needed within himself or close at hand.

As an Irish-theme drama from Neil Jordan, this one is a departure in its nonviolence and its restriction to his home culture, that of the Republic. It may be taken as an overture to his own people, who seemed to be so critical of his films, or it may be that he needed to develop this theme for other reasons. Nonetheless, *The Miracle* stands as his only venture into the realm of the "Dublin realists," filmmakers like Cathal Black and Roddy Doyle. In its grasp of Dublin culture and humor, and its ability to leave the audience feeling hopeful without romanticizing its subjects, this film makes a strong positive contribution to the genre and reiterates Jordan's strength as a storyteller and a character writer. It avoids the cynicism of *High Spirits* and manages to incorporate the faith in the human spirit which underlies *Mona Lisa* while speaking both to the Irish audience and the foreign audience without dipping into the cauldron of the North to do so. Though it was overshadowed by *The Crying Game*, *The Miracle* is, in many ways, a stronger and more coherent statement and paints a truer picture of Irish life. Significantly, it paints a distinctly upbeat picture of Irish society, without resorting to romanticizing imagery to do so; though perhaps slightly tinged with personal sentimentality, *The Miracle* succeeds in capturing some of the best aspects of the Irish character.

A Foot in the Door

Over this century, Ireland has supplied a number of talented actors, writers, and directors to the worldwide film industry, whether based in Britain or California. (Rex Ingram, it may be noted, was one of the first film directors in Hollywood--when Vitagraph Studios moved there in 1916 to avoid Thomas Edison's patent attorneys--and a Dubliner.[4]) It has also provided a wealth of dramatic situations and scenic backdrops, but it has been a long struggle for Ireland to build a community of filmmakers whose collective vision speaks to the Irish people and the themes which interest them. For a variety of reasons, whether they're loved or hated, Jordan and O'Connor have been instrumental in effecting this change.

If one accepts that there are, broadly speaking, three fundamental ways in which to categorize film product--as art, entertainment industry, or propaganda--then a certain set of constraints follows rather naturally. Firstly, since filmmaking is labor intensive and equipment intensive, it follows that any given project must have access to rather large amounts of money for its completion. This typically means that the dilemma facing television also faces film: it is likely to be either commercial (profit motivated) or subsidized by some benefactor (government or private sector). Secondly, if it is either commercially funded or subsidized, the likelihood of censorship (whether for purposes of propaganda or fear of giving offense to potential audience members) increases. Thus, art cinema is left on the fringes of the financial exchange, whatever the source of funding.

This is the dilemma faced by those Irish filmmakers who have aspired to a career in the industry (meaning the multinational industry, wherever one may think it is located). However we may feel about the content of the film work of Neil Jordan, he has made a mark in world cinema and thereby raised the profile of Irish film talent as a whole. Though some of those in the film community in Ireland may begrudge him his success and access to Los Angeles studios and funding, and though he may have made films about complex and sensitive issues in ways that were not as deft as they might have been or in ways that may have been seen by some in Ireland as misrepresentative, he has made films for the world market and, in so doing, proved that Irish talent was up to that task.

Though both films garnered some negative comments on both sides of the Atlantic and from a number of quarters, *The Crying Game* and the subsequent *Interview with the Vampire* clearly demonstrated Jordan's ability to direct and write for the mainstream market. Equally clearly, Stephen Rea and Bob Hoskins benefited from their work with Jordan, and their subsequent success has reflected well on him too. Despite the criticism and despite the occasional utter failure, Neil Jordan has persisted in two objectives: to make films that have a market in the mainstream of commercial cinema, and to bring real Irish issues and viewpoints into some of those films. In this effort, he has certainly eased the way for those who followed--most notably Jim Sheridan--and, whether some of those in the Irish filmmaking community approve of it or not, a substantial debt is owed both to him and to Pat O'Connor for their contributions in this regard.

Notes

1. Published in the United States as *Nightlines.*

2. Marina Burke, "Celtic Dreamer," *Film Ireland* (April/May 1993): 17.

3. Burke, 19.

4. See "Silent Master," *Film Ireland*, (April/May 1995) for a biographic profile of Ingram.

CHAPTER SEVEN
SHERIDAN AND COMPANY

The First Step: *My Left Foot*

If there may be said to have been a miracle in recent Irish cinema, it must be Jim Sheridan and Noel Pearson's leap into the world's consciousness in 1989 with *My Left Foot.* The film itself is not miraculous; it's very meticulously crafted and acted, and the tangible result of much skill and hard work. What is exceptional about it is the fact that neither Pearson nor Sheridan had made a feature film before. Both men came from theatrical backgrounds, and neither was connected with the film industries of Britain or the United States.

The project began with an adaptation of the book of the same name, Christy Brown's autobiography, into a script by Shane Connaughton. Both Sheridan and Pearson had come to feel an affinity with the story; it seemed to reflect the sort of working-class values and trials they identified with the old Dublin culture, and thought that it would play on the international stage. Pearson had met Daniel Day-Lewis (who was born in Ireland, though he--like Kenneth Branagh--is widely considered a British actor) at a theater party in London, and managed to get the script to him. When Day-Lewis had read it, he agreed--over his agent's objections--to play the lead role, and the project then had both a star to draw audience and enough credibility to draw backers.

It then fell upon Jim Sheridan's shoulders to make the film happen. He'd had a solid career as a fringe director in Dublin theater, and a stint at the Irish Arts Center in New York, during which he had also studied filmmaking.   As an Irish-trained director, he had approached drama as a literary device, and language as "a defence mechanism to define territory."[1]   What he learned while working in New York was the need for language to communicate, for a film script to obey a fairly simple structure:

> Screenplays are more like architecture than art in the way that they convey to the readers important information on which they have to act. It is very difficult for them to be self-reflective. They need a structure like a building that people can work in.[2]

He and Connaughton constructed *My Left Foot* as a traditional three-act play--a structure which Sheridan notes was abandoned by most Irish writers early in the century. As such, it made an excellent vehicle for the mainstream film audience: the seemingly insuperably tragic burden into which the protagonist is born, the heroic struggle, and the final reward. It was an emotive and finally uplifting story, and its success stands as a tribute to the architectural talents of its author and director, and the fine performances of all the cast members.

My Left Foot is a true story: Christy Brown was born into a poor family in 1950s Dublin, prior to the advent of the National Health system and just ahead of Sean Lemass's economic reforms. This was especially unfortunate for him, because his father was a .construction laborer and he was born without the use of his arms, hands, or right leg. He also had difficulty speaking, so that he was thought to be mentally deficient, and was relegated early in his life to the status of a vegetable.

The first part of the film deals with this childhood (in which the role of Christy is played magnificently by the child actor Hugh O'Conor), and with Christy's struggle to make his family understand that he is cognizant of them and the world around him. He finally does this by scrawling a word ("mother") on the floor with his left foot--the only limb he can articulate.

Gradually, we see him beginning to develop rudimentary speech skills and to cope with the world.   The closeness and supportive tenor of the Dublin family is shown throughout this; Christy playing soccer in the alleyway (he plays goalie, lying on his side) and experiencing romantic disappointment--all the while being encouraged and defended by the closely knit group of siblings.

This is not to say that the family is idealized. The father (Ray MacAnally) is temperamental and frequently drunk; he starts brawls in the pub and is fired from his job for throwing a brick at the foreman's head. The mother (Brenda Fricker) keeps the family together, stashing away money for the times when the father is unemployed, and standing up to him during a violent tirade when one of the daughters announces that she is pregnant. It is a picture of a rough-and-tumble family life, and probably not far from the reality of the poor urban families of the time. (The sons, for example, sleep three in a bed.)

They are all tenacious and argumentative hangers-on, but Christy is the best of the lot. Despite his handicaps--or because of them--he persists in two most unlikely fields of endeavor: writing and painting. More than that, he succeeds. Indeed, he is shown in the film to have been the most successful of his family, in the end marrying an attractive nurse whom he's met at a charity function, and around whom the "present tense" narrative revolves.

As a storyteller, Sheridan shows great skill. The film opens to a painfully slow shot of Brown putting a record on a turntable with his left foot, and slowly dropping the arm down onto it. It's a great hook for audience interest, and it draws us right away into the kind of empathetic frame of mind he needs us to adopt for the piece to work. From then on, the story is told in flashbacks, returning often to the "present"--the charity function at which Christy is the guest of honor. There are thus two story lines: the interplay between Christy and the nurse at the charity gathering in the estate house of a wealthy Ascendancy[3] nobleman, and the story of Christy's past, presented to us as the nurse reads his book while keeping him company.

Sheridan got his architecture right. As most of us know, *My Left Foot* was a runaway success, both as a commercial venture and as a vehicle for the propulsion of many people's careers. Daniel Day-Lewis has been featured in many films made since, and Jim Sheridan has become something of an old hand in the commercial film community. Brenda Fricker, who played the mother, has worked steadily since, both inside and outside Ireland, and it is a virtual certainty that Ray MacAnally would have seen similar results had he not suffered an untimely death.

This film had a great impact on the market for Irish subjects; the mix of endearing charm and rough realism proved a potent one. The presentation of the Irish as something other than the familiar stereotype was a bold move in terms of international marketing, and yet it was a resounding success. Sheridan did this by playing up the characters' individual strengths against the standard "drunken lout" type without wholly disposing of the hard-drinking image the audience was accustomed to seeing. The hard drinker in this film, though, is the father; his children all show promise of achieving greater success in life, and are shown to be a bit embarrassed at the antics of the older generation in the pub following their father's funeral.

One of the stronger points made in the film is the depiction of that generation gap. As Ireland began to emerge from the isolationist mantle, so the younger Irish saw the prospect of a brighter economic future for themselves. Christy, of all the children in the Brown family, is the most prone to excesses of drink and emotion; nonetheless, these excesses are clearly portrayed as weaknesses, and it is his ability to deal rationally with the disappointments of his life--in times of sober reflection--that gets him through it. Certainly the most heroic figure is that of his mother, who manages to control (or fend off) her husband's mood swings and fiscal irresponsibility and keep the family together and solvent, and who rescues Christy from his most severe funk by building him his own room in the back garden in which to paint and write.

Unlike many of the other Irish filmmakers we've seen thus far, Sheridan has stayed much more within the constraints of conventional structure and thereby given the world audience the sort of fare it has become accustomed to seeing in the cinema. His packages are much neater--the loose ends nearly always tied up, and he seems much more clearly to be making statements than his counterparts. *My Left Foot,* apart from being a tightly structured tale, seems to be more of a vehicle for statement than, say, *Pigs* or *Traveller.* Without resorting to characters' speech-making or undermining the plot in any way, Sheridan has defined for us an image of the Irish culture of the 1950s (and thereby in the relative safety of a period piece) as one in which the combined fear and anticipation of sweeping socioeconomic change is faced by the coherent family unit, a structure which is held together and whose weight is borne by the women. This society is a matriarchy--the older men still somewhat inclined to excessive drinking and still rather adolescent in their behavior and largely dependent upon the women to keep them on track and carry the family emotionally and, on occasion, financially. The question posed in the background to all this (although the film never really asks how Christy will fit into the larger society, if in fact he will) is whether the upcoming generation will find a new structure for itself.

The Field

There is something basically American about the way Sheridan makes movies. His time in New York theater was quite apparently a powerful learning experience, and his film work shows it. If we are to say that *My Left Foot* owes some small debt to films like *Down the Corner* and *Pigs,* then we must say that Sheridan's second film, *The Field,* owes a rather large debt to John Ford.

The Field is set in the years before the Second World War, in which the emergence of Ireland from its self-imposed isolation was dimly visible over the horizon. Structurally, this is as near as we're likely to get to an "Irish Western"; in atmosphere it resembles nothing so much as the American Westerns dealing with conflicts over land and grazing rights--a common theme for conflict in those films. The setup for the conflict in *The Field* is precisely that--the clash between those who regard the land as something sacred and those to whom it is merely property.

The field of the title is a small scrap of reclaimed bogland which one man, "The Bull" McCabe, has built into a fine pasture by dint of backbreaking work--hauling seaweed (for fertilizer) on his back up the cliff face every day of his life. McCabe (played by Richard Harris) is obsessive about his field, and about the need to pass it along to his rather lazy and noncommital son Tadhg (Sean Bean). The problem is that Bull doesn't own the land--he rents it from a widow, whom Tadhg and his idiot friend "Bird" routinely torment for amusement. Finally, the widow can take no more and decides to leave, putting the parcel of pastureland on the auction block.

Enter the villain, a wealthy American-Irish man played by Tom Berenger. The American declares his intention to buy the land and pave it over for a roadway to a quarry. This is sacrilege to Bull, and he calls in all his resources to fight for "his" field. There are a number of side issues and subplots at work which give an Irish flavor to the piece, but the driving conflict is between Bull and the American, and it follows the pattern of the classic Western. After several very public conflicts in the town square, Bull and Tadhg arrange a showdown at the river with the American. It's intended to be more of an ambush and to merely frighten, but the American proves more than a match for the soft and irresolute Tadhg, and Bull finally steps in to finish the fight and kills his adversary.

As a representative of the tough poor farmers of the mountainous coasts of the West of Ireland, Bull is an icon to the other villagers; these are the descendants of the people who survived the Famine years--succumbing neither to starvation nor mass emigration. Lest we miss this point, the script repeatedly expounds upon the Famine theme and the theme of betrayal as felt by those who were left behind to face crushing poverty when the Famine had taken its toll.

During the Famine years (roughly 1845-1850), several splits erupted in Irish society. Although there was no failure in other crops, the potato, upon which the poor tenant farmers survived, was affected with a killing blight, causing the starvation of roughly a million people and forcing the emigration of another million and a half or two million.[4] Other crops, such as wheat, were still being exported to Britain by the Ascendancy (Anglo-Irish) landlords, and many tenant farmers were evicted for nonpayment of rents.   In all this, a rift between the haves and have-nots opened which has still not healed in some parts of the country.   Out of that time the "tinkers"[5] were created--evicted tenant farmers who still travel the roads and are largely condemned by the landed country people who mistrust them. Also, the Church tended to side with the landlords during the Famine, and the Irish who emigrated to England and America eventually turned their backs upon those who remained.

All these sores are probed in *The Field.* The landed aristocracy is represented by the widow, who is an "outsider" and has never actually worked the land herself. Played by Frances Tomelty, she is a thin and frail-looking recluse who still wears black mourning clothes after twenty years. When she finally leaves the village, it is to the taunts and curses of the villagers, one of whom even throws mud at her back. The priest (Sean McGinley) lives in a rather well-appointed house in marked contrast to the squat stone cottage in which Bull and Tadhg and Maggie McCabe (Brenda Fricker) live. Finally, the American (Berenger) is an archetype of the "Returned Yank": fancy fedora hat, leather coat, and brash attitude. He drives a car, in contrast to the native Irish, who travel by horse cart.

As the symbol for the obsessive tenacity of the poor small farmers of the Irish West, Bull McCabe confronts these threats to his way of life headlong. An errant donkey, belonging to the tinkers, strays onto the field and is killed and tossed into a lake for its transgression. The widow is driven out of her house, and the American and the priest are both threatened with violence if they stand in Bull's way. Bull is an obsessed dynamo, and his character drives the dramatic conflicts throughout. The other villagers are afraid of him, as is his family, and neither the priest's castigation from the pulpit nor the local garda[6] (police) sergeant--nor even the American's money--can weaken the hold he has over them.

Finally, it is his own actions which betray him, and we discover at the end that this is not the first time it's worked out that way. Bull and Maggie, his wife, haven't spoken since their older son, Seamus, died twenty years earlier, apparently driven to suicide by Bull's harangue. In the end, Tadhg decides to run off with the despised tinker's daughter (Jenny Conroy), and in doing so drives Bull into a fit of rage. At the same time, the American's body is being hauled out of the lake where it was deposited next to the donkey. As his life is coming apart, Bull drives his cattle over the cliff into the ocean, and drives Tadhg over with them, putting the finishing touch on the collapse of everything he values. At the end, he is shown raving at the sea, slapping at the waves with his walking stick as he wades further out, probably to his own death.

This film was adapted from the stage play of the same name by John B. Keane, celebrated publican and playwright from County Kerry. Keane has long written plays dealing with issues of importance to country people--a fact which meant that his plays were not widely seen nor produced in Dublin for many years. This is indicative of one of the divisions in Irish society, and Keane is certainly well aware of the way in which these factions were divided. There is also a generational split in the country, evidenced by the decline in the use of the Irish language, and *The Field* plays up the fact that the young people in the village cannot understand the Gaelic-speaking "island people" whom they regard as foreigners.

Then there's the division between the Irish and their emigrant cousins. The American in this story is both a subject of ridicule and one held in awe (largely of his wealth) by the villagers. The country Irish have their term in English ("Returned Yank"), which refers with contempt to this sort of person, who often returned home to flaunt his success in the faces of those he'd left behind. (In Irish Gaelic, he would be called "an Puncan mor ramhar," which means, literally, "the big fat Yank" and reflects the perception of those left behind by those who emigrated west that their cousins in America are both rich and soft.)

In this respect, however, Sheridan took some liberty with the original stage play. As written by Keane, the returned cousin was British, rather than American, and the play was set in the 1960s. It is probable that the character was changed in order to tailor the part for an American actor and thereby target the film more directly toward a U.S. audience. While this may well have been good marketing, or even essential to obtain production funding, it illustrates the conflict between the two sides of Jim Sheridan's approach--in which he attempts to straddle the fence between issues of interest to the Irish and to the world audiences. In a very fundamental way, it alters the nature of the conflict. As a dialectic on the subject of Famine politics and its aftereffects, the fact that the intruder is not British is significant. To some extent, the Irish are still in conflict with the British over these issues, at least in the minds of many Irish men and women. This is particularly true in the western countryside, where issues of the Famine and the 1916 Rising and the subsequent Black and Tan War are still hotly felt, and because of which there is still support for the Provisional IRA in the North. By making the villain American and placing the action firmly in the past, the focus of this anger is shifted, and the meaning of the conflict changed and perhaps weakened. It was certainly felt to be the case by some in Ireland, who regarded this alteration as a serious distortion of reality.[7]

Nonetheless, the film works as a tragic drama on the Western-movie model. Although the script tends toward stilted dialogue and frequently slips rather improbably into history lectures (notably in pub conversations and Bull McCabe's tirades), Sheridan and his cast manage to keep the character conflict and the ensuing dramatic tension predominant, and the momentum of that keeps things rolling over the rough spots.

As an example of its type, this story tends toward the melodramatic, and away from character depth or complexity. Bull is a force driven by singleminded obsession, and the other characters likewise tend to exhibit a single characteristic rather than any great complex mix of personality traits. None of them grows in any significant way either; to the end, they persist in their single traits, each characterized by a significant fatal flaw which brings on the tragic end. Finally, this is a very polemical piece whose purpose seems to be to debate the issues of internal conflict inherited by the modern Irish from the festering sores of the past. While that debate has meaning to the Irish audience, its significance would tend to escape the audiences in Britain and America, and the failure of *The Field* to approach the critical success of its predecessor *My Left Foot* may, in part, be attributable to that fact. Try as he would to play up the dramatic conflict between his characters, and despite its inherent structural similarity to an American Western tale, the diffusion of the essential conflict by the insertion of an American in place of the British interloper and the inherent obscurity (to those outside Ireland) of the issues of history underlying that conflict mitigated against the success of *The Field.*

In the Name of the Father

If *The Field* was a departure from the form and formula which made *My Left Foot* such a success, Sheridan's next project was back in that mold. *In the Name of the Father* put him back in the international spotlight and seemed to confirm that the success of his first film was no accident.

This film was, however, a departure from the Sheridan/Pearson team. The collaborators this time were the Irish actor Gabriel Byrne, who coproduced, and the expatriate Irish writer Terry George, who coproduced and wrote the script. The story is largely a factual one, based upon the experiences of a group of people (some Irish and some English) known as the Guildford Four, who were falsely convicted of the bombing of a pub in Guildford, England, during a Provisional IRA campaign in 1974.

In this film, Sheridan returns to the structure which worked so well in his first effort: a narrative (again a male protagonist telling his story to a woman) illustrated with flashbacks. In this case, it is Gerry

Conlon telling this story to a Mrs. Pierce, an English attorney who believes he is innocent and has taken up his case in order to get a retrial. Once again, Sheridan has returned to Daniel Day-Lewis for his lead actor, and this time he's got Emma Thompson to play opposite, in the role of the attorney.

The story is structured in three acts again, and tells the tale from Gerry's point of view. It begins in his hometown, Belfast, during the intense rioting and warfare of the early 1970s. Gerry is a street punk and small-time thief who makes a few pounds here and there by stealing metal (lead and copper) from roof flashings and selling it for scrap. He is fired upon by the RUC (Royal Ulster Constabulary--the police in Northern Ireland) and threatened by the IRA, who are the unofficial police in the Catholic ghetto. After a particularly bad run-in with both organizations, his family sends him off to London to live with an aunt. On the way there, he encounters an old friend, Paul Hill, and the pair of them decide instead to move into a hippie "squat"[8] with another friend from Belfast. While there, they argue with one of the English hippies, and finally decide to leave. Sitting in a park deciding what to do next, they encounter an old homeless man named Charlie Burke, who claims the bench is his and shows them his initials carved into it as proof of possession. (This encounter will prove critical later.)

Aimlessly wandering, they meet a high-priced whore, who drops her keys as she's getting into a car. Gerry takes the keys and enters her flat, stealing 700 pounds. He and Hill split the money and Gerry goes back to Belfast. Soon, he and Hill and several others from the squat are arrested, and taken to London for interrogation, apparently on the testimony of the disgruntled Englishman with whom they had argued. They are all charged with terrorism and held under the recently enacted Prevention of Terrorism law (which gave the British police virtually unrestricted power of arrest and detainment in such cases).

While in police custody, they are beaten, verbally abused, and threatened until each of them breaks down and signs a confession. Gerry holds out until one of the police, an RUC officer, threatens to go

to Belfast and kill his father. This was not a threat to be taken lightly;
rightly or wrongly, it has been widely believed by the Catholic
population in Northern Ireland--as by some independent
observers--that some officers of the RUC were also involved in the
Protestant (unionist) paramilitary organizations and thus could easily
have been capable of acting upon such a threat.

In any case, after a trial which is highly emotionally charged and
rife with political pressure, the "Four" (Conlon, Hill, their friend
Paddy Armstrong, and his girlfriend Carole Richardson) are sentenced
to 30 years in prison. Also sentenced (to varying terms) are members
of Conlon's family, including his father and his aunt, whom the
government claim to be part of a network of spies and bomb makers.

The second "act" of the film deals with Gerry and his father
Guiseppe (Pete Postlethwaite) adjusting to prison life and to each
other. They had never been close, Gerry resenting his father's manner
and the fact that, because he was Catholic, he'd always held
subservient jobs. Guiseppe had, in fact, been ill much of his life due to
a lung disease acquired while working as a painter in one of Belfast's
ship factories. It is made plain in the course of the dialogue that these
hazardous jobs were the only ones Catholics could get in those
shipyards (which are virtually the only industry left in Belfast).

After a great deal of angst and rebellion, the two men come to
terms with each other. Guiseppe is becoming increasingly weaker,
and Gerry becomes his friend and nursemaid. Eventually, of course,
Guiseppe dies, and in the third act, Gerry finally becomes truly angry
and decides to focus that anger. Mrs. Pierce, who had been consulting
with his father for some time, now gains Gerry's full confidence and
support, and together they bring to fruition the public relations
campaign which she and Guiseppe had been orchestrating. In the end,
it works: the pressure of public outcry brings about an appeal hearing,
fifteen years after the convictions.

Quite accidentally, because of the illness of the police archivist
assigned to work with her, Mrs. Pierce is able to see some confidential
files which prove that the police did interview Charlie Burke--that
homeless man in the London park. The statement taken from him by

the chief inspector, a Mr. Dixon, has also been clearly labeled "Not to be shown to the defence." In the final triumphant trial scene, she produces the evidence of the police cover-up (and the corroborating evidence of the confession, obtained after the Conlons' conviction, by the man who actually executed the Guildford bombing). The judge summarily throws out the charges, and the Guildford Four walk away free. A footnote to the film tells us, however, that Guiseppe Conlon was not absolved and the police and their supervisors were never disciplined.

This film is unlike *My Left Foot* in its clear objective to make a political statement. (In fact, it makes several.) In that, it is more akin to Sheridan's second film, *The Field,* but without the obvious lecturing which seems to bog down that script. He has, in this instance, managed a balance between the politics and the human-interest drama which works especially well for the non-Irish audience. (The Irish were not so enthusiastic, for reasons we'll encounter later.)

Probably due in large measure to the writing style of Terry George, who is a journalist, *In the Name of the Father* manages to keep its edge as a story of social injustice and political intrigue. The facts of the case are laid out clearly and sequentially so that we understand the complexities involved, and the relentless pursuit of justice by Emma Thompson's character carries the sort of righteous crusading banner with which we can all identify. In reality, as we'll see, the facts were embellished a bit--but the essential truth of the Conlons' innocence was not. In that context, this film has the pace and feel of a good investigative thriller--reminiscent, in fact, of *All the President's Men* (the film about Washington *Post* reporters Woodward and Bernstein and the investigation of corruption in Nixon's White House). George manages to deal with the Northern Ireland situation in a way which is much less simplistic than in many another film of this kind, such as *Patriot Games* (although even *Cal* or *The Crying Game* may be seen to present the Northern situation in a way that understates its true complexity), without compromising the essential dramatic appeal of the story.

7. *In the Name of the Father:* **Jim Sheridan and Terry George create the paradox of a box-office success that is openly critical of the British presence in Northern Ireland.** (Copyright 1993 by Universal City Studios Inc. Courtesy of MCA publishing rights, div. of MCA Inc. All rights reserved.)

That dramatic appeal seems to be Jim Sheridan's forte, and he works it with aplomb in this film. The thread that ties things together throughout the piece is the first-person slant: as with *My Left Foot,* we're encouraged to empathize with the protagonist. We feel his fear when the full weight of the British political and military machinery comes down on him, the horror at being sentenced to prison knowing one's own innocence, and the final rage which grows out of years of injustice. We feel Mrs. Pierce's loathing for Dixon, who she knows is lying to her, and her excitement at finding the suppressed evidence. Finally, we feel the rush of exultation felt by all the innocent victims at their vindication in the concluding scenes.

Rather than focusing on a conflict between two characters to drive his story along, as he did in *The Field,* this time Sheridan uses Gerry Conlon's singular struggle to keep the energy levels high. Initially, it is Conlon's personality, that of a daredevil street punk seemingly at odds with society in general and his family in particular. Later, it is his conflict with the forces of authority in London. In the course of the story, he changes from a reckless rebel to an heroic figure with a mission, and part of the dramatic interest of the film is the reason for that change.

It is, of course, his treatment at the hands of the British police. As a rebellious hippie, he was unfocused and seemingly only interested in Jimi Hendrix music and the pursuit of his own pleasure. While this generates conflict between him and his father, it does not seem to us, as outside observers, any reason to condemn him. As an Irish youth in London, he's also quite naive, and the combination of these qualities adds up to a personality unable to muster interest in political issues and certainly ill-equipped to orchestrate a terrorist attack.

Thus, the police who arrest and intimidate Conlon, and ultimately fabricate evidence against him and the other defendants, are shown to be the products of a corrupt system of institutionalized thugs. The veneer of British gentility and politeness is depicted as a very thin one indeed, and the scenes of interrogation are akin in brutality to those of *Midnight Express*. There was some resistance in Britain to this portrait of their police, who have long been regarded as a highly restrained and civilized force; nonetheless, the facts of the case were well documented, and it seems that the powers granted the police in the Prevention of Terrorism Act may well have been abused. (This writer was, on several occasions in the 1980s, the subject of a stop-and-search policy implemented under that law and applied randomly to Irish-registered cars on British roads.) Taken on a personal level, that sort of experience turns the film, for that segment and in that context, into a sort of horror film by inviting the viewer to imagine himself in such a situation.

Lest the film appear to be a pro-IRA propaganda device, however, a diversion from the facts of the story was created in the form of a character named McAndrew--a captured IRA man, and the one who supposedly set the Guildford bomb. In the story, he is an inmate with the Conlons, and in the course of their incarceration together, he takes Gerry under his wing and begins to politicize him. After McAndrew has become well entrenched in the prison, he mounts an assassination attempt, severely burning the warden with a cigarette lighter modified into a small flamethrower. At this point, Gerry sees him for what he really is and severs the relationship.

It was for this bit of fiction that the film took the most criticism in Ireland. McAndrew was a fictitious character; no such person existed in the true account of Gerry Conlon's prison experience. Although there was an IRA prisoner who confessed to the Guildford bombings, the rest of the details about this character were made up, apparently to add dramatic interest to the prison segment and to dramatize the fact that Conlon was by nature nonviolent. It also served to soften the portrayal of the British and Northern Irish police as unmitigatedly evil, together with the scenes showing the RUC detective who'd threatened harm to Conlon's father expressing regret about the conviction later on, after the real bomber had confessed. (It is significant that he is the only one of the British authorities involved in the frame-up who shows any remorse about those actions. This is consistent with the film's portrayal of the British police as cold-blooded, since he is actually an Irishman.) More importantly, however, it seemed to some Irish to pander to the mainstream stereotype of the IRA as ruthless killers: this apparent retreat into the simplistic may have been seen by some as both an inaccurate choice and one driven by the need to sell the film to a mainstream American audience rather than to paint a truer picture of a very complex situation.

Terry George acknowledged the difficulty of this dilemma, noting that a balance needs to be struck between the desire to deliver a "hard story" and the need to draw an audience from the world market, to satisfy financial objectives.[9]   To be fair, however, the portrayal of the Provisional IRA[10] in this film is comparatively sympathetic in that it refrains from the sort of blanket condemnation present in some other films set in Ireland. In the early scenes of this film, they are seen to be a fairly effective vigilante police force, and the popular support given them in the Catholic ghettos is quite dramatically shown. Certainly, compared with these people, the Provos of *The Crying Game* or *Cal* are demonic in their evil and unrelenting barbarism and portrayed in a manner nearly as two-dimensional as those of *Patriot Games.*

Sheridan, however, is quite clear about his objective. Although this film contains some powerful political resonances, he insists that the essence of it (hence the title) is the development of the relationship between the two Conlons, father and son. He is fairly blunt about that:

> Nobody is really interested in an injustice story. It is a difficult story to tell. But the father and son story is not so difficult.[11]

In this, his approach is consistent with those of Neil Jordan and Pat O'Connor, the other two Irish directors who have addressed the Northern Ireland issue most prominently. As with their films on this subject, *In the Name of the Father* reduces the larger political and social issues to the level of personal dilemma: how does the protagonist deal with his position in this larger conflict? This raises issues of personal moral and ethical conflicts and discourages the audience from distancing itself from those inner conflicts. Again, Sheridan is fairly blunt about it:

> . . . in Ireland we can tell personal stories whereas in Hollywood they tell mass stories for a mass audience. I think Irish filmmakers can fall into the mistake of thinking that they can go into the mass market without losing their identity. I don't think you can unless you are an expert technician and I don't really think that's our bag.[12]

There is a further implication to this statement, and it may well have been intended. As Sheridan noted in a *Film Base News* interview,[13] the Irish have tended to regard language as a sparring tool rather than a device for communication; to enter the mass market, he seems to be saying, they must learn to simplify their stories. The mainstream film market, having been fed for so many years on Hollywood fare, seems to have an appetite for such simple three-act structures, direct-action plot lines, and unembellished language. Certainly the bulk of Hollywood product would tend to reinforce this view, and it does create a dilemma for the Irish writer and director. Sheridan, with his bicoastal hybrid point of view, was able to sum up the Irish literary and theatrical tradition quite neatly and, at the same time, cut to the core of the problem:

> In the best Irish plays nothing happens, and sometimes, as in *Godot*, nothing happens twice. . . . Even [Joyce's] *Ulysses* uses someone else's plot and has the main characters wander through it and think about life.[14]

There is, he believes, a fundamental difference of structure between the Irish storytelling tradition and that which is familiar to and expected by the mainstream film audiences:

> In current American films most writers use a three-act structure that could come out of a play at the end of the last century.[15]

What he is advocating--in fact, what he has himself implemented--is a "retrograde" movement toward the dramatic structure of nineteenth-century realism in order to access the mainstream market. This is Sheridan's solution to the dilemma stated earlier by Joe Comerford--the desire to tell Irish stories and the need to garner funds from outside Ireland to do that. The solution, in this case, would be to compromise structure for mass-market acceptability. It does seem to have worked for Jim Sheridan: two solid successes out of three tries is a phenomenal record in the fickle film industry. Nonetheless, there are those in Ireland who would say that the compromise is too great, and that the essence of a story's Irishness may be too heavily compromised in order to make it fit the alien mold. It is certain that the reaction to the McAndrew character was a strongly negative one--possibly because it was a fabrication which went against the facts of the story--but also, I think, because it was a Hollywood-style device used to turn the course of the action artificially in a more simplistic, dramatic way.

Still, Sheridan is doing what he set out to do, and doing it with great success. In a strange twist, he (as well as some who went before and have come after) has begun seriously to achieve the goals to which the National Film Studios originally aspired: the wholesale employment of Irish film talent utilizing foreign capital. It is probably important to note that he has done this by approaching film from a creative angle rather than an industrial one, the lesson being that to achieve success in the film industry, one must have a command of the art form first--a lesson that the Irish government never really learned, only coming to terms with it on the heels of *My Left Foot*'s commercial and critical success.

Shane Connaughton and *The Playboys*

As I mentioned at the beginning of this chapter, the person who adapted Christy Brown's book into a screenplay was the writer Shane Connaughton. Just as Sheridan and Pearson were able to spin the success of *My Left Foot* into other work, so the critical acclaim it garnered for Connaughton has generated further film projects for him.

The first of these was *The Playboys,* a feature produced with American money and directed by a Scotsman, Gillies Mackinnon. Though *My Left Foot* was his first feature film, Connaughton had long been writing for television and has since gained further prominence as a novelist. Like Neil Jordan, he writes most often and best about his home country, the northern counties of the Republic which lie on the border with Northern Ireland. His most recent novel, *The Run of the Country*, has been adapted into a screenplay and is in release as I write this.

Like *The Run of the Country, The Playboys* is set in a small village near that border. Like any small Irish village, the mix of personalities and close proximity in which they must live makes a sort of dramatic cauldron from which many a story could develop. This particular one revolves around the intrusion into such a community by a band of itinerant players (a particularly ragged troupe of actors who call themselves "The Playboys," presumably after the John Millington Synge play) during a summer week, and is further fueled by the village's proximity to the border and the cultural and political overtones that interjects.

As with *My Left Foot,* this film has the cushioning device of a 1950s setting to distance it from the political and social realities of the present. The central character is a young woman, the local shopkeeper Tara (played by Robin Wright), who has conceived a child out of wedlock and thus scandalized the village. In a portrayal which may be slightly revisionist, she is both proud and defiant, refusing to give the child up and refusing to name its father. This is the same dramatic device Roddy Doyle used for *The Snapper,* but in this case the heroine has no strong family to support her, with the exception of her sister Bridget (who is little more than a background figure).

The situation is further complicated by the presence of an older, but nonetheless ardent, suitor in the person of the local garda (police) sergeant, played by Albert Finney. (This is a character who figures prominently in *The Run of the Country* and Connaughton's book of short stories, *A Border Station.*) There is another suitor, a farmer named Mick (Adrian Dunbar), whose cattle mysteriously die and who commits suicide early on in the story.

There is a suggestion that the sergeant may have had something to do with Mick's demise, and it certainly seems as though Tara will have to submit to his pressuring eventually, the way having thus been cleared of all other competitors. But then the Playboys arrive.

Heralded by the arrival of one of the company, a brash young actor named Tom who rides into the village square on a motorcycle, the troupe moves in and sets up its ragged tent-theater. As with the travelers, these people are regarded with suspicion by officialdom, and generally live by their wits. It becomes evident that they make very little money by honest labor, and it is no great surprise when Tom is caught by Tara stealing one of her chickens. This begins his fascination with her, and his pursuit of her, around which the bulk of the story turns.

Inevitably, Tom and the sergeant become rivals for her affections, although it is quite evident that she really feels nothing for the sergeant. As she grows closer to Tom, the sergeant becomes more insistent and intrusive, until finally he tells Tom the big secret: he is the father of the child. This only deters Tom momentarily, and it becomes clear that he and Tara will end up together.

Meantime, the other players are going about their various businesses. Freddie (Milo O'Shea) is the leader of the troupe and a failed actor from Dublin with lofty ideas and some extreme delusions of grandeur. Rachel, the fading leading lady, takes money behind the tent to bare her breasts for the local men (a pound to touch them) while her husband and son are onstage inside. And Cassidy, the mysterious Northerner, is quietly making bombs and sneaking off to unknown places to plant them.

As the lovers cement their relationship in a barn, the company of players goes off to a nearby town to see *Gone With the Wind* in the cinema. Faced with tangible evidence of their ultimate demise, they resolve to go back to the village that night and re-create the film onstage. It is destined to be laughable, and made more so by the absence of Cassidy in the Rhett Butler role; Tom, who has not seen the film, is forced to ad lib the part. (Cassidy, we learn later, is off on more "IRA business.") While the players' performances in the town square have thus far been dreadful, their treatment of this story is outrageous: each performer playing multiple parts, in drag or blackface, and a truly hilarious final scenic effect of the burning of Atlanta in which we expect the tent itself to burn down.

As the crowd roars with laughter and applause, the sergeant bursts into Tara's house to find Bridget and the local blacksmith in a compromised position on the sofa. Enraged and intoxicated, he steals the baby and the village square erupts in a ruckus. Several of the village men take the baby from him, and he and Tom square off for a fistfight. Tom wins, but the sergeant gets up and wrecks the tent theater before breaking down in tears.

Suddenly, it's the next morning, and we see the sergeant in civilian clothes, boarding a bus with suitcases in hand, leaving the village for good. Then Tara appears, kissing her sister goodbye before boarding Tom's motorcycle to ride off with the company of players, several small boys running down the road after them as they disappear over the stone bridge.

With this film, Connaughton has constructed a microcosm of Irish society on the cusp of greater change than it had seen in many years. In the middle 1950s, the prospect of emergence into mainstream culture was just beginning to be realized, and the old ways of doing things were on the verge of being ushered out.

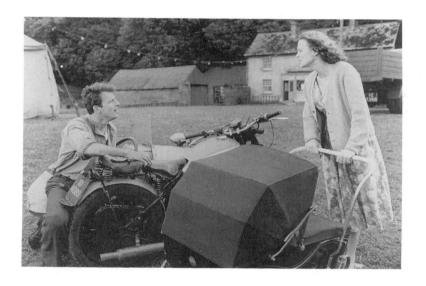

8. *The Playboys:* **Shane Connaughton's allegory of change in rural Ireland.** (Copyright 1992, The Samuel Goldwyn Co. All rights reserved.)

The small village shown to us, with its inward-looking and very authoritarian worldview, was about to be torn apart by the intrusion of outside cultures and the wholesale change of Ireland's economic structure. We're reminded throughout how it was in these places: in the background of every shot are several villagers, just standing and watching. Even when Tara and Tom make love in the players' caravan (trailer), there is a gaggle of old men standing there to watch it rock in the rhythm of their lovemaking.

The threat to the players posed by the cinema is coupled with scenes of the gradual incursion of television as another symbol of the intrusion of the new age. Tara and her sister run a shop and do sewing and tailoring work, but Tara also smuggles goods across the border, risking arrest by the Republic's customs officers in the process. On one of her smuggling runs, she encounters another smuggler who shows her a television set and asks if she knows what it is. "Wireless with pictures," she says. Later, we see the village publican erecting an antenna and trying out his new black-and-white TV in the bar. Still later, the villagers are shown gathered at the bar or peering in the windows at the new contraption, and we know then that the players' days are numbered as are the days of the old way of life in these villages.

Tom and Tara symbolize those changes. As the film opened, we saw Tara's water breaking in the middle of Mass, and the priest's look of condemnation as she and her sister Bridget hurried out. As an unwed mother--but most especially an unrepentant one--Tara represents a challenge to the authority of the Church. Her actions and attitudes bespeak a disregard for that authority and for the sort of closed, stiff, prudish society under which Irishmen and Irishwomen lived until relatively late in the century. As the parish priest is trying on a new pair of trousers that Tara has sewn for him, he makes a few slightly lewd comments, perhaps foreshadowing some of the revelations to come years later, when society would permit the transgressions of priests to be openly discussed--even in Ireland. (Remember I said that this may be a revisionist look back at the past-- it is most certainly one informed by knowledge of subsequent events and changes in society.) In a final dismissal of the religious dilemma, however, there is an offhand blasphemy spoken by one of the villagers during a community hay-pitching session in which Tom and Tara and the baby arrive on a donkey: "Will you look at that--Jesus, Mary, and Joseph!"

At its core, this is a story about the disruption of the old order by the new. Although the Playboys are a dilapidated band of has-been actors and themselves represent a vestige of the past, they also represent those who live outside the bounds of respectability and the reach of law or church. They bring with them a delicious kind of craziness--a reckless abandon and disregard for the things that settled people value--which makes them dangerous. They also serve, in this case, as a vehicle for Tom, who proves to be an important catalyst in Tara's life, and the sergeant's, and by extension the rest of the community.

As an omen for the future, the players carry the seeds of everything that is to come for Ireland.   Cassidy represents the reignition of the Troubles in Northern Ireland, which had settled somewhat in the years following the Second World War. The players all show a flagrant disregard for the civil authority of the sergeant, and they even best the priest in the realm of mysticism when an old blind lady recovers her sight at one of their performances. Coupled with the concurrent arrival of the television, the film gives us a pivotal week in the lives of these villagers and a dramatic event that is symbolic of the way their lives (and those of others in similar villages all over Ireland) would be altered a few years hence. The final shot is carefully constructed and very important to the meaning of the film: not only is it a nostalgic look back (shot, as it is, from the point of view of a person in the convoy of departing vehicles) at the long-lost past, it leaves us with the image of several small boys chasing excitedly after something they find enticing--their backs turned on the village. We know, of course, that this scene will be repeated later, when those boys are men, and then their departure will be permanent.

The Legacy of the *My Left Foot* Team

The combined talents of Sheridan, Pearson, and Connaughton contrived to raise world awareness of the Irish and some of the issues important to them.   As stereotype-bashers, they have been exceptionally successful, and may claim a large share of the credit for the filmmaking "boom" now going on in Ireland. Although the three were only together for the one film, that single effort generated enough spin-off work to make each of them (and more than a few others associated with them) significant players in the Irish and international film communities.

What was achieved, particularly by Sheridan, was a means of access to the mainstream industry (in Los Angeles) combined with a retention of the "Irishness" of story content and an Irish base of operations. Despite their groundbreaking work, both Neil Jordan and Pat O'Connor have had to relocate their operations outside Ireland at one stage or another. Though Jordan has resolutely returned to Irish subjects when he could, projects like *Mona Lisa* and *Interview With the Vampire* have diluted his image as a director associated with Irish subjects. Apart from *The Crying Game,* Jordan's Irish films are largely unknown to the mainstream audience. *My Left Foot* and *In the Name of the Father,* however, are not.

Sheridan, as we know, had spent some years in New York, learning the vocabulary (both linguistic and dramatic) of the cosmopolitan. Pearson had, as a theatrical producer, built a proven track record of stage productions that had a mass appeal. (His production of *HMS Pinafore* was quite a success in Ireland and England, taking full advantage of the expiration of D'Oyly Carte's "contract" on Gilbert and Sullivan in that year.[16]) Finally, Shane Connaughton had experience writing for British television, which particularly suited him to make the adaptation of Christy Brown's story to a mass market.

Jim Sheridan's understanding of the need for such adaptation and his command of the architecture and language required to effect that adaptation has ensured his success. In that sense, the teaming of his talents with those of Terry George, who has been living and writing in New York for some years, made perfect sense for *In the Name of the Father,* and proved essential to its appeal to the American audience. The British, though they flocked to see it, had some difficulty rationalizing it, as they have with most Irish films: They called *My Left Foot* a British film because of its commercial success, and *The Field* Irish because it flopped. *In the Name of the Father* gave them difficulties because it was a commercial success, yet identifiably Irish, even anti-British.[17]

It will be quite interesting to follow the further exploits of these creative talents. They have demonstrated to the larger film community and, more importantly, to the Irish film community, that it may be possible to strike a balance between the demands made by Hollywood to garner financial backing and the need to make genuinely Irish films. Essentially, they are faced with the dilemma with which Joe Comerford and others making "art films" have had to grapple: the conflicting demands of funding (from outside sources, necessarily) and aesthetic/cultural integrity. As Comerford and Jordan know, there may not be a "happy medium"; it is rare that the Irish audience (at least as embodied in the Irish critical fraternity) is fully satisfied with the results of these compromises. Nonetheless, much work has been done through their efforts to present Irish stories, characters, and issues in the multinational venue in such a way as to dispel some of the stereotyped and oversimplified preconceptions which have predominated heretofore.

What all of them have achieved--and the common thread through all their work--is the telling of "personal" stories. One of the advantages of being Irish today is a sense that (probably because of the compact size of the country) no one is inaccessible and no idea unassailable. Taking on large issues and reducing them to the personal is not a difficult thing to do if one is raised in that mind-set, and it is a hallmark of most of the work discussed herein. Jordan, O'Connor, Sheridan, Comerford, Black, Quinn, McArdle--all have used this device to good effect, together with a comparatively literate approach to subject matter.

One last comment from Jim Sheridan may serve to explain another fundamentally Irish approach to filmmaking, and one born of both its verbal tradition and the age of its culture:

> In essence, I don't think film is a predominantly visual medium. It's just a storytelling medium with different aspects; one is visual, one is sound, one is music. The visual tends to predominate because it is the most powerful, but it's not necessarily always the most true. Film is more a medium that manipulates concepts of time, I think.[18]

Notes

1. Jim Sheridan, "Words, Pictures, and Buildings," *Film Base News* 12 (April/May 1989): 11.

2. Sheridan, 10.

3. The term "Ascendancy" refers to the old monied/landed classes in Irish society--typically Protestant, though not uniformly so.

4. Readers may find Tom Murphy's play *Famine* of interest, as well as Patrick Kavanagh's poem *The Great Hunger.*

5. These are the travelers discussed in chapter 5.

6. The Garda Siochana (literally "guardians of the peace") are the police force in the Republic of Ireland. They are usually unarmed, and govern largely by social pressure and persuasion rather than the threat of physical harm.

7. Point made by Kevin Rockett in a panel discussion at the Walter Reade Theatre, Lincoln Center, New York on 26 June 1994 during a season of indigenous Irish films presented by the Film Society of Lincoln Center and the Film Institute of Ireland, and organized by Kathleen Murphy and Sunniva O'Flynn.

8. A condemned or abandoned house in which homeless people live illegally (see chapter 5).

9. Remarks made at the same panel discussion in the Walter Reade Theatre, New York, 26 June 1994.

10. I refer throughout this text to the IRA, Provisional IRA and "Provos": these all refer to the Provisional Irish Republican Army, which sprang up in Northern Ireland in the 1970s, as distinct from the "Old IRA" of the 1916 Rising and Civil War of the 1920s. The Provisional IRA is an outlawed organization in both Northern Ireland and the Republic of Ireland.

11. Hugh Linehan, "Getting Out of Jail," *Film Ireland* (December 1993).

12. Linehan, "Getting Out of Jail."

13. Sheridan, "Words, Pictures, and Buildings," 10.

14. Sheridan, "Words, Pictures, and Buildings," 11.

15. Sheridan, "Words, Pictures, and Buildings," 11.

16. For many years, the D'Oyly Carte theater company in London had reputedly been able to dictate the production style of all staging of Gilbert and Sullivan in Britain, under the terms of the performance rights. Noel Pearson had presented a highly irregular (and extremely entertaining) production of *HMS Pinafore* in Dublin just prior to the expiration of this provision in Britain. The production was transferred to England immediately after its Dublin run.

16. Remarks made during the panel discussion at the Walter Reade Theatre, New York, 26 June 1994.

17. Hugh Linehan, "Getting Out of Jail," *Film Ireland* (December 1993).

CHAPTER EIGHT
IN AND OUT OF THE MAINSTREAM

A Time of Change

In cinematic terms, Ireland may be said to have emerged from its isolated status largely within the past two decades. Prior to the 1970s, the only film production of any size to come out of Ireland was foreign product which (as Pat Murphy lamented) simply used the country as a scenic backdrop for stories that could, in most instances, have been transplanted anywhere, so generic were their themes.

For the first time in recent history, we have begun to see films with Irish themes coming from the efforts of Irish writers and directors and addressing issues of concern to an Irish audience. This may be seen to be a development on par with the Rural Electrification Scheme of the 1950's (which brought electric power to every farm and hamlet across the Irish countryside) and the formation of the Industrial Development Authority (which encouraged foreign companies to set up operations in Ireland, rather than keeping them at arm's length as had been past practice). Neil Jordan, Pat O'Connor, and Jim Sheridan have all proven that Irish talent can find creative success on the world screen; having done that, there can be no easy retreat. The tendency of the Irish government to try to restrict the growth of filmmaking in Ireland and the widely accepted stereotype which relegated the Irish to "cottage industries" have both been challenged by the sheer presence of such talented people in the world marketplace. This is yet another arena in which Ireland can be said to be emerging, and doing it with the vigor of people who have been kept waiting in the wings too long, and are now ready to claim their place. (This may also be seen to parallel the emergence of Ireland as a primary source of musical talent and as the "silicon valley" of Europe.)

Far from the situation which predominated when Ardmore Studios opened in 1958 (when the need to train film technicians was supposed to have been addressed), there are now several colleges in Ireland offering solidly structured programs in film--often in the context of art rather than technology. The graduates of these programs are entering the marketplace now; they produce short films, work on commercials and feature films, work in video production. Some of them leave Ireland for jobs in Britain or the Continent, but many are staying at home, and they want to make films there about their culture and their concerns.

No doubt they will. They have the benefit of having much of the way cleared for them. The limited mainstream success of certain Irish directors and writers and the political savvy and unceasing agitation of others has at least made a space in Irish society for these newcomers to fill--a space, significantly, which did not exist before.

Roddy Doyle, Alan Parker, and *The Commitments*

Certainly the most explosive commercial and critical cinematic success to come from Ireland was the film made of Roddy Doyle's novel *The Commitments.* The timing, formulation, and writing of this film were nearly perfect, and enable us accurately to characterize Doyle's subsequent rise as meteoric. He had dabbled in playwriting prior to this, but without feeling that it was entirely his medium.[1] Still, his published playscripts (*Brownbread* and *War*) clearly indicate that he had a good sense of absurd comedy, comic timing, dialogue, and character construction. In both plays we can see the roots of *The Commitments*' success: the clash of Irish and American cultures, the sardonic Dublin humor, and the quirky characters who would make the film so popular.

For those who might have missed it, *The Commitments* drew its humor from the reality of northside Dublin life. The Rabbitte family (not a made-up name, by the way) are fairly typical of the inhabitants of Corporation housing: relatively poor (though that is changing), nominally Catholic, and a bit rough around the edges. They also, for various reasons, are fairly well attuned to American culture--at least as it is exported by American industry. Thus, it should be no surprise that the father, Jimmy Sr. (Colm Meaney), is an obsessive fan of Elvis--to the point of conspicuously placing Elvis' portrait above that of the Pope in the family sitting room. ("Elvis is God!" he remarks at the breakfast table, and it is taken as no blasphemy in the Rabbitte household.)

This story, however, is really about Jimmy Jr. (played by Robert Arkins). Jimmy Jr., unlike his father, has more cosmopolitan musical tastes and no job to occupy his time and energy. Thus it is that he decides to become an entrepreneur and take over the management of his friends' floundering dance band, "and and! and." His plan is to create the first Irish soul band, on the premise that the Irish, as the last colonized people in Europe, have a position which parallels that of African Americans. ("The Irish are the blacks of Europe," he says--a line which is used to good effect whenever a quizzical frown is the desired response.)

The film then proceeds, tongue firmly in cheek, to show us how that premise could come to some measure of success. The band becomes tighter and begins to make some money, even coming close to signing a recording contract. In the end, though, egos and infighting break them apart (as they do most popular bands) and the musicians go their separate ways, leaving Jimmy Jr. rather disconsolate but philosophical about it all.

Throughout, the script is peppered with Dublin wit and brashness. The utter cheek required to conceive of such a venture is a very Dublinesque characteristic, and the unflagging sense of the preposterous in every aspect of life (whether it's rehearsing a soul band in a Dublin pool hall or living in a tiny concrete-walled flat with a half-dozen squabbling children, as Bronagh Gallagher's character Bernie does) provide ample opportunities for verbal and visual humor which is both accessible to a larger audience and particular to the Irish experience. There is such a profusion of gags in this piece, and on so many levels, that the jokes which the English and American audiences may have missed because of an unfamiliarity with inner-city Dublin dialect were overshadowed by the sight gags running more or less simultaneously with them.

It may also be significant that the film was directed by Alan Parker, a Briton, and thus may have been tempered a bit for the untrained ear. It is to his credit, however, that the film follows the book quite faithfully; obviously, Doyle was an active participant in the filming, as the portrayal of Dublin life attests. There is an underlying truth to the characters in this film which shows through those aspects that have been exaggerated for comic effect. Despite the fact that they're largely poor, they are possessed of an understated dignity and a disrespect for inflated self-importance which has seen many generations of poor Dubliners through some very hard times. These people are the heirs to the inner toughness of the tenement-dwellers of Jim Plunkett's *Strumpet City* and James Joyce's *Dubliners*. They have little to lose and few illusions, and the sheer flamboyant preposterousness of Jimmy Jr.'s plan for the band is testament to both qualities.

Doyle has subtly worked other elements of Irish culture into this piece. The strong attachment to American culture is obvious in the musical taste of the Rabbittes; that it is a product of strong physical and familial ties between the Irish and their cousins in the United States is given tangible presence in the form of Joey "The Lips" Fagan, played by Johnny Murphy (who has frequently appeared in indigenous Irish film productions). Joey has performed (or so he claims) with all the great soul and R&B musicians in the 1960s and 70s--a claim which may be unlikely but is surely not impossible (viz, Van Morrison, a poor boy from Belfast).

The strong family, which is not uncommon in Dublin, is also

shown clearly here. (It's worth reiterating that the book upon which this film was based was the first of a trilogy of novels about the same family, the common theme among them being the nature of the Irish working-class family and its positive interrelationships.) There is a kind of offhand casualness about the Rabbittes, and a detached bemusement at Jimmy Jr.'s exploits, but the criticism only goes as far as sarcastic ribbing; they may think he's a bit loony, but they all seem to wish him well. These are energetic and eccentric people living in very cramped circumstances, and Doyle gives us a portrait of such a group managing to defuse the tension with humor and to be supportive and loving without being smarmy. There is, however, another side to Irish family life and the brief scene in Bernie's (Bronagh Gallagher) Corporation flat gives us a glimpse: an older woman still having babies, insufficient income to support the children who're there already, and an absent father. There is certainly no shortage of such dysfunctional families in Dublin, but in this instance (as distinct from the later film, *Family*) Doyle has chosen to focus on one that works.

Indeed, despite the run-down scenery against which the action takes place, despite the cynicism which runs throughout the humor and the ultimate failure of the band's hopes, there is a note of optimism reserved for the finish. It is partly the realization that Joey's summation is correct ("This way, it's poetry") and partly the way that the individuals salvage something for themselves from the wreckage that makes this an upbeat film. Some of the band members (the more unlikely ones) actually make careers in the music business, and others find a new enthusiasm for other life paths, but for all of them the experience seems to have been something of a turning point.

The film was also a turning point in Irish-theme cinema. Although produced and directed by people outside Ireland, it managed to remain faithful to its subject. Notably, although the crew heads were largely British, there were no American or British actors featured, and few concessions (if any) were made to the predominating foreign stereotypes. Despite criticism from the home ranks (as long as films are made about Ireland, they can be expected to offend some element of Irish society), this film was imbued with a sense of truth:

watching it, one had a sense of knowing these people already, of having met people quite like them in Dublin. Nowhere in *The Commitments* is there a sense that it is portraying to us or to the home audience an image of Irish life the way it ought to be; rather, it seems to be showing us several aspects of the culture as it exists, and making no apology for that.

9. **"Oy, Ginger!" Roddy Doyle and Alan Parker make *The Commitments*, an allegory of urban change**. (Copyright, Beacon Communications Corporation. Courtesy of Beacon Communications Corp.)

In that respect, this film does what *My Left Foot* didn't: it shows us what it may be like to be young and living in Dublin today. There is none of the mist of nostalgia nor the buffer of a period setting to soften the issues. The young people in this piece are very like some now living in Dublin--they face limited job prospects, a strong likelihood of forced emigration or of forced marriage and early parenthood. These are hard prospects and will require some hard choices, but their ability to imagine something better and their energy and humor stand them a chance, at least, of making something better for themselves. What *The Commitments* has done, then, is to present some of Ireland's thornier problems in the context of a very witty and strongly personal story--very like other work by indigenous talent, such as Cathal Black or Fergus Tighe. The difference with this film, and the privilege it granted to Roddy Doyle, was that it gained access to the world market for one of these "realist" voices.

It would be wrong to conclude that the people and situations presented in this piece are representative of the whole of Irish life. In the suburbs of Dublin are many middle-class families who live quite well by anyone's standards, and there are those in still other parts of the country who face none of the hardships presented here. Still, Dublin constitutes the greatest concentration of population in Ireland, and a significant share of Dubliners live in circumstances like those Doyle portrayed in this film. What may serve the Irish well in this instance is the presentation to themselves and (more importantly) to the world outside Ireland of a population of Irish people who vary wildly from any of the stereotypes, and whose existence on-screen challenges the larger world to question the veracity of those stereotypes.

My Left Foot, The Playboys, Widows' Peak, and *Circle of Friends* all fit rather neatly into the mold of a quainter, softer image, however much they may have introduced elements of greater truthfulness into their portraits of Irish culture. *The Crying Game* and *In the Name of the Father* both tapped into the violent image of the Irish already forefront in world perception. *The Commitments* did neither; it managed to show a wide diversity of characters, a culture in tune with and well aware of the world culture around it, and people whose lives, though far from violent, yet have a sharp edge that makes them interesting.

Strongbow Films: *Eat the Peach*

In a very real sense, a debt is owed to a film from the '80s that established similar character types and also addressed the modern Irish situation in a realistic manner. This too was the product of an English director (although one who had worked in RTE and was himself a bit more in tune with the Irish), Peter Ormrod, and an Irish producer, John Kelleher. The film was called *Eat the Peach,* and was made in 1986.

Unlike the young people whose lives are central to *The Commitments,* this film revolves around a slightly older group who are better educated and, until the opening scene, gainfully employed. That opening depicts a gathering of Irish people employed by a Japanese multinational corporation (of some unspecified scientific/manufacturing nature) who are assembled to be told that they're all to be laid off. This has, unfortunately, been an all-too-common occurrence in the past several decades as foreign companies came to Ireland to take advantage of tax benefits and packed up and left as soon as the benefits ran out. They've been Japanese, American, Canadian, and German predominantly, and their negative impact upon the Irish who worked for them has done much to tarnish the images of those countries in Ireland.

That said, the film then picks up on the lives of two of these people, Vinnie (Stephen Brennan) and Arthur (Eamon Morrissey). Here we have a different sort of dilemma: two people of a high degree of education and skill left with nothing to do. They've been paid a fairly sizable severance packet and are entitled to unemployment benefits, so they're not destitute. Still, they've got nothing to occupy their time. They do go to the pub, but drinking doesn't adequately pass the time, although it does provide them with an idea. Vinnie sees an old Elvis Presley film on the pub television which inspires him to build a "wall of death" in his own back yard. (A wall of death, for those who might not know, is a circular structure with vertical walls around which a daredevil rides a motorbike sufficiently fast that the bike is perpendicular to the wall--parallel to the ground--thus "defying gravity." It is, simply, a carnival stunt.)

10. Toasting the "Wall of Death" in Peter Ormrod and John Kelleher's ode to harebrained schemes, *Eat the Peach*. (Courtesy of Samson Films)

Preposterous though this idea is, Vinnie and Arthur dive into it headlong, scouring the countryside for lumber and ordering outrageously tacky daredevil costumes to wear during the big show. They are faced with two big problems: Vinnie's wife (played by Catherine Byrne) moves out, and the two entrepreneurs run out of money. To realize the project, they enlist their friend "Boots" (Niall Toibin) to manage their venture, and go to work for his crooked boss smuggling untaxed gasoline across the border from the North.

This provides opportunities for some comic antics, themselves a bit preposterous, which help to pass the time until the wall is built.

Boots runs afoul of his employer (he has, apparently, been watering
some smuggled whiskey and taking a cut for himself) and is trussed up
in traction at the local hospital on the big day; but despite his absence
his public relations efforts work out well: the event is attended by a
prominent politician and an RTE camera crew, and is aired on the
evening news. Unfortunately, the wall proves a little too flimsy, and
the audience perched atop it (led by the politician) runs away in fear of
its life. So the great carnival show comes to nothing; in despair and
frustration, Vinnie sets the whole thing on fire.

His wife and child do come back to live with him, and we're given
an epilogue scene at the end in which we're told that Boots survives
the gangsters and that Vinnie becomes a tomato farmer. But there's
that mysterious lumpy thing under a tarpaulin in the yard: it turns out
to be a helicopter that he and Arthur are building from old car parts.
As the rotor begins to turn, Paul Brady sings, the camera elevates, and
the credits roll, leaving us with a sense of the indomitable spirits of
these slightly crazy friends.

Eat the Peach was made by two television producers from RTE,
and there is a certain look and feel of a television piece about it. It got
some airplay in Ireland and abroad, and had a small cult following in
the United States, but failed to be a hit of any nature and failed to
make Strongbow Films, its production company, a significant player
in the world market.

There is some nice comic writing, both in visual gags and
characters, and a laudable attempt to address some real issues and to
portray modern Irish culture in a way that is closer to the truth than is
usual. Ireland is shown to be a marginal player in the world economy,
and a frequent victim of the whims and changes of the multinational
corporations. This story clearly shows the impact a giant company
can have on a small country--what is merely a reshuffling of resources
to such a corporation can have a devastating effect upon the life of a
whole community.

Importantly, it also depicts quite clearly the ambivalence many
people in the Republic feel toward the North of Ireland; to Vinnie and

Arthur, it is quite plainly another country and another culture. In one scene of the two of them smuggling gasoline, their wagon (with a tank of gasoline disguised as a load of hay) and tractor are blown up by British troops as they take shelter in a pub full of paramilitaries. The people in the pub are quite threatening, and the two men from the Republic quite fearful for their lives, not knowing on which side of the Northern political divide they've landed. The image of the North presented here is one of a strange and dangerous place, but a place that may be exploited for the financial gain of those outside it. Nowhere is the rectitude of that assumption questioned.

Like Jimmy Rabbitte Sr., the "Boots" character is an Amerophile, wearing cowboy boots and ten-gallon hat and talking in a laughable drawl as he lies about his exploits in the States. In Irish usage, the term *cowboy* means someone who bluffs his way through life claiming to know how to do things without really knowing. Boots is a cowboy in both meanings of the word, and a good comic figure, if a bit too broadly drawn. He is symbolic of the man who has to pretend to be more than he is, but fails miserably to convince anyone around him.

In the main, *Eat the Peach* is about dreamers. Faced with circumstances beyond their sphere of influence, which have soured their expectations of comfortable and productive careers, Vinnie and Arthur fall back on their ability to dream to salvage hope. There is something endearing about that, but also something childish and self-centered, and it is the latter that causes Vinnie's wife to leave. The bad guys are truly ruthless and vicious; lovable or not, Boots is soundly beaten and nearly killed when he transgresses against his boss, and the politician is clearly portrayed as a criminal up to his neck in dealings with gangsters.

Some real, difficult aspects of modern Irish society are shown here without too much embellishment. Unemployment (even for the highly skilled), impotence in the face of multinational companies, political corruption, and the decay of the agricultural economy are all here. No realistic solution, however, is forthcoming: the epilogue leaves us with some rather improbable ones, tomato farming and helicopter manufacture. While *Eat the Peach* was a bit hard-edged, even for 1986, and its efforts to show Irish society a bit more clearly were laudable, it finally is a frivolous piece, leaving these subjects with an improbable upbeat ending, and finally using most of its imagery for comic effect rather than posing any serious questions.

It has been a difficult task, trying to bridge the gap between films that speak directly to Irish issues and those that might also appeal to the foreign audience, and the way is fairly littered with brave but failed attempts to do so. Another of these was screened in March 1994 at the Dublin International Film Festival and again, three months later, at the season of Irish films shown at Lincoln Center in New York.

Maurice O'Callaghan: *Broken Harvest*

It is one of the sad facts about Irish history that few outside Ireland are familiar with it. Certainly it is not widely understood in either the United States or Britain, even among the large populations of Irish descent which reside there. Many are unaware that Ireland had a civil war, even though that is quite likely the single event in recent history which has had the most profound effect on Irish culture.

One of the holdout areas of the "diehards" (those who refused to accept the Irish Free State in lieu of a republic) was the western rural part of the country. Logically, this was where some of the most bitter battles were fought in the Civil War, and where the most bitter feuding was carried on after the war was over.

The Civil War and its aftereffects, both political and personal, make a good source of dramatic tension, and it is natural that filmmakers might want to build a story around those events. One such was Maurice O'Callaghan who, with his sister and brother, wrote and produced *Broken Harvest,* which is entirely structured around the conflicts arising from that war and its subsequent repression in the public mind.

The story deals with two farmers, on opposite sides of the conflict and suitors for the same woman, whose repressed hatred is played out years later in the 1950s. The plot is tied up with several country traditions, such as public reading by the priest of parishioners' tithes and communal assistance between farm families with harvesting chores. Understanding of the delicate balance of social life in an Irish farm community is crucial to understanding of the story; hence, this film was fated to be largely inaccessible to any audience outside the culture of rural Ireland. In an apparent attempt to counteract this, the film's producers wrote a number of rather stiff speeches of information into the dialogue, which turn parts of the film into thinly veiled history lessons during which action and character development grind to a halt.

The effort was a doomed one from its inception; nevertheless, it serves quite well to illustrate a serious problem shared by much film product to have come out of Ireland. Much of what is dramatic for the Irish is misunderstood or simply overlooked by foreign audiences. The balancing act required of an Irish filmmaker who would also hope to enter the world market has a lot to do with this dilemma, and is tied quite strongly to the difficulties faced in raising production capital.

Some films, notably *My Left Foot* and *The Crying Game,* managed to attract worldwide audiences and still say something to the home audience. The former did this by using a story that had powerful elemental emotionalism built into it; the second by utilizing a blend of political statement and salacious sexual imagery whose unfortunate effect was to obscure much of the meaning of the piece to those outside the Irish culture.

Joe Comerford: *High Boot Benny*

In The Name of the Father and *The Crying Game* used the notoriety of the violence of the Northern Ireland conflict to draw a world audience share; Joe Comerford's most recent effort (also given its U.S. premiere at Lincoln Center in June 1994) although set amid that conflict, uses it in a different way and makes a very different sort of statement. *High Boot Benny*, perhaps Comerford's cleanest and most effectively structured film, still possesses the edginess and bleakness of *Traveller* and *Reefer and the Model*, his other two films which deal with the North.

Benny (Marc O'Shea) is a young Irish punk--Mohawk haircut and high boots--living in a rather unorthodox independent school located just across the border in the Republic. The school is run by a former priest (Alan Devlin) and a matron (Frances Tomelty), with assistance from Benny, and is populated largely by children who seem either to be unwanted or problematic. Educational freedom is a theme underlying the film--and is closely allied to Comerford's empathy for marginalized groups in Irish society generally.

The school is also a bit of an island of calm amid the chaos of cross-border military activity. There are British soldiers and RUC (Northern Irish police) illegally crossing the border to arrest or assassinate people they suspect of IRA membership as well as genuine IRA people making forays into the North. It is a high moral plateau in a landscape of violence and subterfuge: no one among the locals will admit to involvement with the IRA, but they all seem to be sympathizers, if not active members. The staff of the school, Benny included, are resolutely divorced from all that, until Benny interferes with a supply of blood being surreptitiously carried from the local doctor's surgery to a hideout where an IRA man lies wounded. The Provos take revenge, tarring and feathering Benny and tying him to a telephone pole.

Ultimately, it transpires that the priest in the school was in league with the IRA, and both he and the matron are brutally killed in one of those illegal cross-border forays by the RUC. Benny escapes, by hiding in the rafters and watching silently as his two friends bleed to death below. This is enough to politicize him, and the film ends with the funeral scene in which Benny leaves with the IRA supporters.

High Boot Benny might have been little more than an adventure film, but this director could not have done that with it. The hallmark of Comerford's films has been a strong sense of poetry; although he has shown us thieves and smugglers and killers, he has also been resolute in his refusal to treat them two-dimensionally or to make them predictable.

11. Out of place: Marc O'Shea plays Benny, an urban punk thrown into the violence and confusion of the Border in Joe Comerford's unsettling *High Boot Benny.* (Courtesy of the Irish Film Archive and Joe Comerford)

Thus, though it has all the right elements, the film never takes an easy road. The IRA are never portrayed as either good or bad; they are merely shown to be doing what they do. The staff of the school strive to stay above the conflict around them, but one among them is flawed--he is certainly played as the weakest member of the group--and the result of that is the destruction of everything they've worked to build. In its collapse, though, the school reminds us of the frailty of independent thought in this world of conformism. There is nothing more frightening to the forces of conflict and control than an

independent thinker, this film is saying, and finally Benny is forced
into submission: he ends up taking sides.

    Joe Comerford has achieved something unusual with *High Boot
Benny*, and although it hasn't achieved commercial success, it has
become a feature of a number of film festivals in Europe and the
United States. It is a film that many people need to see; it is, as one
reviewer in New York said, "edgy and dangerous." It succeeds in
demonstrating the dangerous nature of ideas--no mean feat indeed.
    Additionally, it is quite beautifully shot.   The whole film is
suffused with a poetic bleakness--a cold and stony landscape in which
Benny and others come and go surreptitiously.   The opening scenes
are shot with a quality of surrealism; nighttime at a military
checkpoint on the border as Benny smears a "Welcome to Northern
Ireland" sign with the blood of a dead rabbit.   The underlying
tension--whose root is the unspoken network of subterfuge with which
everyone lives but to which no one refers--never lets up and we begin
to feel just how difficult it must be to maintain the pacifist line of
thought in such a climate.   This is not a film about bloodshed; it's
about conflicts of ideas and the emotional toll they take, and it shows
just how much more powerful are these subjects than are the overt acts
of violence which so often pass for drama in films.
    Benny may also stand as a representative of modern Irish youth.
He certainly looks like the young people to be found in the cities of
Ireland, in such areas as Dublin's Temple Bar district. Many dress in
punk uniform--black leather, punk haircuts, and pierced body parts
abound--and there is an underlying sense of mistrust for authority
which seems to run deeper than the usual adolescent ennui. There is a
sense among them that their political and cultural leaders may not be
trustworthy; that the old guideposts have lost their relevance. As such,
Benny is a misfit in the rural north; there, the old conflicts are still
being played out with little tolerance for those whose predilection is to
run at a tangent to the old way of thinking.
    Young men like Benny are largely products of the Republic,
where they've had the luxury of isolation from the Troubles. The

politics of the Northern conflict are not an important part of their lives, and in a real way they symbolize much of the population of the Republic, whose attention has long since turned to other matters. In this context, *High Boot Benny* raises the spectre of another sort of conflict having to do with Northern Ireland: the prospect of what may happen to the people of the Republic if they are once again drawn into the violent politics of the North.

Joe Comerford: *Reefer and the Model*

Prior to *High Boot Benny,* this film was Joe Comerford's most ambitious work. Much of *Benny* is informed by it, and they share similar settings, both geographically and politically. In overall tone, *Reefer and the Model* is less "dangerous" than its successor: although more obviously meant to shock, it is also imbued with a wry humor which helps to take the edge off some of the political and social comment and to distance us from the situation.

Completed in 1988, it made the rounds of film festivals in Europe and was given a run in Dublin and London. In Irish filmmaking circles, it generated a great deal of talk and controversy--in that, it probably succeeded more than any of Comerford's other works in doing what its maker wanted it to do. *Film Base News,* the Irish film journal which has since been replaced by *Film Ireland,* published a series of panel discussions, called "Reefertalk," involving various members of that community through several of its issues. Although picked up by Hemdale Films for U.S. distribution, *Reefer* never got much exposure here.

Structurally, it's a bit difficult to follow for those accustomed to the standard three act format. Like *The Crying Game,* it's really two stories welded into one. The first is a sort of road movie, peopled by strange characters about whom we really know nothing. Chief among them is Reefer (played by Ian McElhinney), who we later learn is a fisherman working off the coast of Galway, where the film is set. (His nickname, as it happens, derives both from "Reef"--the name of his trawler--and from his penchant for smoking marijuana.) Driving with his aged mother along a country road, he picks up the Model (Carol Scanlan), who is hitchhiking. After a couple of stops along the way, their trip brings them to the boat, where the Model moves in and we meet Reefer's two partners, Spider (Sean Lawlor) and Badger (Ray McBride). Straight away, they set sail for Kilronan, on Inis Mor (the largest of the Aran Islands) with a cargo of mixed goods and two passengers.

The Model, apart from having been a prostitute and junkie, is also pregnant. Thus Reefer's boat becomes a kind of last-chance haven for her, and Reefer and his friends a sort of surrogate family. They begin to settle into an unconventional domestic life, when impending financial disaster and an urgent need to set sail (fueled by an encounter with an unfriendly army sergeant in Kilronan) rekindle among the men an inclination to resort to their old means of survival--bank robbery. Spider's IRA past and Badger's transvestism stand them in good stead as they hold up a small country bank branch, although things subsequently go awry when a Garda giving chase is killed in the crash of a squad car.

At the point of the robbery, the film changes modes and becomes an outlaw adventure, changing pace as it does so. Despite their clever underground hideaway (which reveals where Badger got his nickname), the IRA man and the transvestite are tracked down by a squad of armed Gardai, and Spider is left dead and Badger in prison. At this point, things fall apart: with the aid of Reefer's old mother (and her Old IRA pistol) the Model puts to sea, where she is to rendezvous with Reefer in a rowboat. Overcome by labor pains (brought on by the exertion of starting the trawler's engine), she inadvertently runs Reefer's rowboat down, leaving him floundering in the water. She ties the trawler's wheel with a piece of rope, and screaming in pain, slumps to the floor of the wheelhouse as the boat drifts and the credits roll.

Despite an apparently fractured structure, this film hangs together, largely by means of the strong thread of a love story which runs throughout. It is put together like a Wenders road movie in the first half and a Hollywood chase film in the second, both of which seem incongruous in the context of an Irish setting. The scenery is as incontrovertibly Irish as are the people--a collection of quirky and difficult odds and ends from various episodes in Irish history. Reefer has aspirations to Gaelic nobility (complete with a contempt for the monied classes clearly articulated in one outrageous restaurant scene). The Model is a hooker and drug addict in a country which had long denied the existence of such people among its own--and exiled her to England, as it has many another errant Irishwoman. Spider is a depoliticized IRA man (who has nonetheless not relinquished his penchant for bank robbery) and Badger a cross-dressing homosexual in a Catholic culture which denies his right to be there. Finally, there's Reefer's mum--the sweet old lady with a revolver and die-hard politics who asks the young policeman whom she's holding at gunpoint, "Is there a prison for old republicans?"

These are Comerford's people: those who have been marginalized because of some element of their character which doesn't fit into an "acceptable" image of Irish society. Just as they are out of place in their own country, so, in its way, is this film. The use of narrative structures which seem alien in the Irish landscape underscores the differences between Irish ways and those of the outside world, as it also points to contradictions within Irish society.

One such contradiction is clearly and poignantly drawn in a Kilronan dance hall sequence, in which Badger is discovered in a sexual liaison with a soldier of the Republic. A brawl ensues when Spider makes a stand for his friend against the soldier's sergeant. The conflict is interrupted by Reefer, who later throws the sergeant overboard when he finds him skulking around the boat. Like outlaws in an American Western, these misfits know the code of mutual defense, and stand against the forces of "polite" society as represented, in this instance, by official intolerance of homosexuals. It is significant that the locals (Gaelic-speaking island people, here representative of the original pre-Christian culture) don't seem to be particularly disturbed by the gay men's behavior--it is only the army sergeant (an interloper on leave from border-patrol duty, and representative of modern urban Irish culture) who's upset.

Reefer's stated aspiration to be a "Fenian aristocrat" harks back to an historical truth (somewhat obscured by subsequent nationalist rhetoric) that leaders of past nationalist movements have, in fact, been members of the Protestant aristocracy.[2]   His disruption of the restaurant in an upper-crust country club may be taken, in this context, as an assault on the "new ascendancy" and their affectation of the manners of the old upper classes.

Finally, the Model represents the antithesis of the woman's role as sanctified domestic, the Madonna of de Valera's mythos of the happy Irish family--as does Reefer's mother.   Hard-nosed and streetwise, hooker and addict, the Model manages to find a sort of love with Reefer, and she provides him and his two partners with a focal point--something to give their lives a greater purpose and direction, however tentative and fragile it may be. Both women are shown to be quite different from their outward appearance: Reefer's mother is still the hardened guerrilla fighter of the Black and Tan War beneath the outwardly helpless guise of an old lady, and the Model is still very naive and vulnerable despite her hard exterior.

12. An unlikely band of outlaws: Ray McBride, Ian McElhinney, and Sean Lawlor in *Reefer and the Model.* (Courtesy of the Irish Film Archive and Joe Comerford)

Reefer is itself an assemblage of contradictions. It is a road movie that abruptly changes direction, an adventure story that never reaches a conclusion. It's a love story that leaves the fate of the lovers hanging. Does Reefer drown? Does the Model regain control of the boat? Is she giving birth or having a miscarriage? No answers are given or hinted; we're left out in the bay treading water as abruptly as we were shunted from one plot structure to another, and without apology. The point is there, though, hidden among the questions.

Comerford is helping us to reach a conclusion, in a very circuitous way, but it's not about what happens to the individual characters. On one plane, he's helping us to formulate an image of an Irish identity by showing us what it isn't. It isn't the sort of thing that makes a good road picture or outlaw film: it can't be packaged that neatly. It may be a love story, but it's a prickly, difficult one which doesn't necessarily have a happy ending. To the world audience, he may be saying that whatever Irish culture is, it isn't what we imagine. To the Irish audience, he's prodding them to question their assumptions about their own society, challenging them to take a serious look at their own history, at their social institutions, at their values, and ask themselves if their country is going the way they want it to.

This is a difficult film, full of hard questions to which there are likely no definitive answers. Its intent and its effect is to be disturbing, but in very specific and focused ways. Principally, it asks who represents Ireland. How should Irish culture and history be presented? Who should be making those representations, and how should those stories be told? It's *Man of Aran*, retold with a rusting old diesel-powered trawler instead of the noble hand-hewn currach--a powerful *woman* forging a kind of optimism from several broken lives by sheer tenacity and strength of will. It's a rejection of the Gaelic idyll as failed fantasy, hinting at the probable triumph and greater nobility of real life--warts and all--over idealized myths. It tells us that our comfortable assumptions have been wrong, but gives us no simple substitutes with which to fill the gaps. This is what Joe Comerford's work is all about; he likes to confront the hard questions, whatever the result:

The phase we've entered into is one of intellectual escapism. The problems we have with the North--with economic and philosophical identity--are so enormous. And faced with having to deal with that, we've opted for denial. It's not just a denial of what's happening in the North, it's a denial of what's happening in the same city you're living in: the drug problems, the poverty problems.[3]

Cathal Black: *Korea*

In terms of confrontationalism, Comerford's closest associate would have to be Cathal Black, who has also been his collaborator on many projects.   Certainly *Our Boys* (chapter 5) stirred some controversy in its time, although Black contends that it would appear tame next to today's headlines:

> I think now, if I'd known it was going to be banned on RTE for ten years, I'd have shown some of the more obvious things that everybody's talking about now. It's almost like a tea party in some parts, compared to what's going on now.[4]

Although *Pigs,* which followed, was a much less obviously contentious film, in its time it also touched some raw nerves and made Black seem still more confrontational:

> Ironically enough, a lot of the less bourgeois or middle-class audiences loved it when they saw it on TV, late at night on RTE. They thought it was right on. But I was lambasted in *In Dublin.*[5] They said it was a downbeat film by a downbeat filmmaker. Dealing with the sexual ambiguity of Jimmy's character--I think some people just didn't like that at all.[6]

Still, *Pigs* was more conventionally structured in its narrative form, and dealt with those contentious issues in the more acceptable context of personal conflicts of fictional characters.   Black's latest effort, *Korea,* continues that trend. It is much more a continuous narrative, and nowhere does it mount a soapbox to make its point. The characters are not misfits or outcasts from their culture, nor are their circumstances particularly unusual.

The film is built upon the scenario sketched out in a very short story of the same name by John McGahern. The film script was written by Joe O'Byrne, a writer and stage director of long standing in the Dublin theater community. The film is set in the lake district of County Cavan among the residents of a small rural community in the early 1950s.

The principal figures are a father and son, John and Eamon Doyle (Donal Donnelly and Andrew Scott), and the story hinges on a critical period in the evolution of their relationship. They make their living eel fishing in the lake, selling the catch for shipment to the East End of London, where it is a highly regarded delicacy. It's not much of a living, and they have a rather austere life out of it, but they're a hard-nosed and very proud lot, and they get by.

The dramatic catalyst is the intrusion of the modern world on this quiet backwater. As the story unfolds, several events happen to upset the balance of things. One of their neighbors' sons is returned home from Korea in a coffin draped with the American flag, having been killed in the Korean War. The Rural Electrification Scheme comes with its wires and power poles and general disruption, and Doyle is served notice that his fishing license will not be renewed.

This last is upset enough (for John Doyle has no livelihood apart from the fishing), but soon a far worse blow is dealt: his son and only child falls in love with Una Moran (Fiona Molony), the younger sister of the slain soldier. Inexplicably, Doyle begins machinations to force his son to emigrate, despite the near certainty that he, like Luke Moran, will be drafted and sent to Korea. The reason behind these actions, we discover, is an old hatred between John Doyle and Ben Moran (Una's father, played by Vass Anderson) dating from the Irish Civil War. As time runs out, and events pile on to turn up the emotional pressure, we see the depth of this hatred--that Doyle would rather see his son dead than married to Moran's daughter.

Finally, after a great deal of internal anguish, Eamon goes against his father. In the end, by the simple gesture of calling Una Moran by her first name, John Doyle finally indicates that he's found the strength to put his animosities behind, and we know things are likely to work out well.

By the very simple cinematic device of cutting strategically to an unsettling shot of caged eels squirming around each other in the murky water, Cathal Black reminds us of the underlying threat buried beneath the veneer of politeness and civility between the older men. We see the dogged resolve of John Doyle, his near addiction to the sparse lifestyle and simple ways of the past, evident in the way he lives: the tenacity with which he argues against electrification, and the simple way he plods, flat-footedly, along the country lanes.

Moran, by contrast, has bought into the idea of a new, outwardly reaching (and more materialistic) Ireland, and lives in an improved and whitewashed cottage by contrast with Doyle's old and shabby one. Moran is involved politically, eager for electrification, and symbolic of the new capitalism under Sean Lemass.

The old men are on opposite sides of the 1950s political fence, just as they were thirty years before. The difference here is that Moran seems to have moved on, while Doyle is still clinging to the old ideology and the old conflict. Of course, the intrusion of the new and foreign moves relentlessly onward, and we know from our vantage point that Doyle will lose if he persists. Both of the young people know this as well, and it is the conflict between this knowledge and the depth of love and respect Eamon has for his father that nearly tears the boy apart. In the end, however, Eamon's love for Una is stronger--sufficiently so that he brings his father at least part of the way along with him. In that slight movement, John Doyle signals the beginning of the end of the old conflict and the cancer it represented beneath the fabric of post-Civil War Irish society.

There is yet a further probe into the psyche of the old rural society. It is rumored among the townspeople that Ben Moran has received compensation from the U.S. government for his dead son, to the tune of several thousands of dollars, and implied that this may have been his intent in allowing his son to emigrate. In line with the time-honored expectation that the emigrant children of the rural Irish would send regular packets of money home (a letter without money inside was called an "empty letter"), there is the assumption among the villagers that Moran somehow made a good exchange of his son's life for a lump sum of cash--not a flattering image at all, and seemingly an indictment of the greed underlying Ireland's embrace of capitalism under Lemass.

13. Still fighting the Civil War: Doyle (Donal Donnelly) and Moran (Vass Anderson) in Cathal Black's *Korea*. (Courtesy of Cathal Black)

It is also indicative of the ambivalence of Ireland's relationship with American culture that no one in the Cavan village really understands the meaning of Luke Moran's death. (Emigration was, until recently, akin to death since few Irish emigrants would ever return.) More significantly, though, it is only Eamon who--plagued with nightmares about being sent to Korea himself--seems to have any grasp of the injustice of an Irish emigrant dying in Korea for the U.S. Army.

By contrast, the depth and intensity of the acrimony carried over from the Civil War is illustrated in John Doyle's actions regarding his son. That it is so important to him may initially be hard for those outside Irish culture to understand, but the film goes a long way toward the explanation of that without resorting to lecturing to do it. The tension between father and son (as between both fathers and their children), although tightly controlled, is palatable and quite powerful; through this, Black shows us on the level of primary emotion how these unresolved conflicts have festered in the psyche and soured the lives of those who carried their sores with them through all the years since the Civil War.

Contributing substantially to the film's power is the sheer beauty of the photography. Together, Cathal Black and Nic Morris (director of photography) have crafted a film that is breathtakingly stunning in its richness of imagery. There is a mystical quality to the atmosphere, and a subtly effective use of graduated filters that serves to shroud the events in a kind of haze but also intensifies the characters' emotional conflicts. In a significant way, the environment thus becomes a player itself, lending weight to the sense that the resolution of Moran and Doyle to end their personal feud is also a triumph over both men's surroundings, which seem almost to conspire against them.

As elegant a portrait of a group of outsiders as *Pigs* was, *Korea* functions on more levels, and with even greater subtlety and eloquence. The writing is consistently believable, and the acting quite understated and compelling. It is powerful and direct, and put together with great skill and understanding of film drama.

Thaddeus O'Sullivan: *December Bride*

On an equal level, as regards the subtle and sensitive treatment of a delicate emotional story, is *December Bride*. As *Korea* delves into the innermost recesses of a rural Catholic village, so does this film plumb the psyche of the Presbyterians of County Down in the last century. Made in 1990, *December Bride* was based on the 1951 novel by Sam Hanna Bell. It is an exceptional film, both because it centers upon a segment of Irish society which has not been the subject of much dramatic writing (and virtually no film portrayal) and because it represents the highly visual quality of O'Sullivan's work and the extent to which he is able to integrate the visual with the narrative.

Trained in art school, Thaddeus O'Sullivan made his name initially as a cameraman and then a director of photography. He worked extensively with other Irish directors, notably Comerford, Quinn, Black, and Murphy, before striking out on his own as a director. That powerful eye for composition and camera dynamics has remained a hallmark of his work--nowhere so plainly apparent as in *December Bride*.

Talking about his work, he speaks of instinctual choices, of composition and texture as extensions of textual meaning and character portrayal. When asked by Luke Gibbons why this film looks the way it does, he answered:

> If I had made that film about a similar story in Kerry, another rural community, the form of the film would have been completely different. The film would have a completely different feel to it, because the way Kerry people express themselves is very different. The camera would have to move differently.[7]

To illustrate that point, just such a contrast is evident between the visual style of *Korea* and that of *December Bride*. While the former is lush, soft, and muted, the latter (while also paced rather slowly) is much more stark and visually sparse--more contrasty. In that, it agrees texturally with the mind-set of the Northern Irish Presbyterians. Settling in Ireland to avoid persecution, they built themselves a closed community, distinct from the Church of Ireland (Anglican) Protestants as well as from Catholic society. Historically, they have even taken a nationalist stance against British rule, and though the important things to know about them in the context of this story are their insularity from those around them and their stubborn independence, the film does go some way toward exploring the frame of mind that would make the same religious community militant nationalists in one century and equally militant unionists in the next. These qualities are reflected in a spare lifestyle (although not necessarily a poor one) and a strict code of behavior, coupled with a propensity for the cryptic verbal expression that borders on high art.

Into this world, then, we have the introduction of a strong-willed freethinking woman, Sarah Gomartin (played elegantly by Saskia Reeves). She and her mother are taken in by a household of bachelors--a father and two sons--as housekeepers. Not far into the first part of the story, set at the turn of the century, the father (Andrew) drowns in a boating accident, notably releasing his grip on the capsized boat's hull in a noble gesture to spare the others. Thus, Sarah and her mother are left to care for the sons.

During Andrew's wake, Sarah takes exception to the rather sanctimonious insistence of the minister that the hand of God has spared her life and those of the two brothers. Rather, she feels certain that Andrew alone was responsible; she saw him let go of the boat, and takes offense on his behalf that an act of noble selflessness should be demeaned by crediting it to God. This is the beginning of a rift between Sarah and the pastor that never really heals.

Eventually, Sarah's mother moves out, in the heat of an argument about Sarah and the two brothers not attending church. Sarah stays on. She has a sexual relationship with Frank at first, out of which a son is conceived. Still, she stays on with the brothers--unmarried--to the consternation of the pastor and despite the ostracism of the community. In spite of social pressure and repeated visits by the pastor (in one of which he makes an awkward sexual overture to her), she refuses adamantly to marry either brother, though she later settles into an informal husband/wife relationship with Hamilton, the older and more charming one.

14. Saskia Reeves and Donal McCann in *December Bride,* **Thaddeus O'Sullivan's film of sexual liberation and feminism in the closed community of Ulster Presbyterians.** (Courtesy of Little Bird Films)

The film then shifts eighteen years into the future, and we discover that Sarah has had another child--a daughter. She and the two men are still living together, and the cohabitation arrangement seems to have worked out quite well. Finally, when her daughter is ready to marry, Sarah succumbs to her entreaties and, as an older woman, marries Hamilton (hence the title of the piece).

As Cathal Black has done in *Korea,* Thaddeus O'Sullivan here uses strong textures in his characters' surroundings to set them off and make his point. As the overgrown, slightly shabby environment of the village in *Korea* was used to good effect to contrast with the incursion of the outside world, so the stark landscape, strong visual contrasts, and pristine orderliness of the Presbyterians of Strangford Lough sets off the complexity of the underlying emotional conflicts.   These surface in the lives of Sarah and her two men, and their power is signified by the violent rejection they receive from the neighbors. (In one significant scene, Frank is beaten and his back broken by the brothers of a village woman whom he has dared to court.)

As a psychological portrait of a people, *December Bride* succeeds in showing us an emotional quality whose defining aspect is its depth. O'Sullivan characterizes these as "people who reveal more than they intend to" thus,

> They don't talk things out, they don't say what they mean. Everything is approached obliquely and quietly, and the film is like that. It never seems to be saying anything, and yet ultimately it is satisfying.[8]

Though the novel clearly portrays the tension in the relationship between Protestant and Catholic in the North, that is played down in the film. (There is a scene in the book--significantly underplayed in the film--in which Sarah demands that a Catholic tenant family be evicted from an adjoining farm after the brothers purchase it.) This film is about quite another aspect of Northern Irish character--the hardheaded independence of a few members of an isolated sector of the larger community, whose sense of individuality extends even to defiance of the moral strictures of their own people. In this respect, *December Bride* is unique in its hands-off approach to this subject: except that it is quite obviously a work of dramatic fiction, it has about it the sense of truthfulness of a good documentary, and thereby a hard-won and quite impressive dramatic power. In that respect, it has much in common with the work of a filmmaker who lives and works in County Down (the locale of this film), John T. Davis.

But first, it's worth taking a look back at another film by Thaddeus O'Sullivan, a black-and-white short shot in Dublin. In 1985, between other projects, he undertook the filming of a short piece based upon a story by Sean O'Faolain. The film features Bob Hoskins and Brenda Fricker as a man named George and his wife, Mary, living in Dublin in the 1930s, and is called *The Woman Who Married Clark Gable*.

The Woman Who Married Clark Gable

George is an unexceptional factory worker whose marriage seems to be slipping. Mary seems to have been caught up in a sexual fantasy about Gable, which is carried to the extreme. She knows all the lines from his films and seems to think that she has some sort of relationship with him. This troubles George until he realizes what the problem is. At that point, he grows a thin mustache just like Gable's, and works a kind of magic on his wife's delusions. She seems convinced that he actually is Gable, and their life then returns to normal.

It is only a short film, and there is nothing exceptional in the story itself, apart from a slightly quirky and quite amusing premise. What O'Sullivan has done, though, is to make it an exercise in the re-creation of the period through lighting and camera control. Through angular composition, 1930s-style chiaroscuro lighting, and strongly backlit shots, he achieves that objective quite faithfully. The resultant piece is both an enjoyable back reference to a time and cinematic style for which the filmmaker seems to have a fondness, and also a brief glimpse of an Ireland between the Civil War and the Troubles; of an Englishman married to an Irishwoman and living in Ireland without any political subtext to it.

In this sort of work, O'Sullivan has found his forte; here is an Irish filmmaker whose first response to a text is visual, and whose interest in things Irish is dominated by the personal:

> I work visually. I will look at a story and see how the locations and
> the background and the world these people live in is going to inform

and how I can best get that across visually. And that's the beginning
and end of it.[9]

John T. Davis: Documentarist

There is another Irish filmmaker whose bias is strongly visual,
and whose eye is drawn to the dramatic. Nonetheless (and perhaps
surprisingly for some) he makes documentaries. Also acutely aware of
American popular culture, he has made a film--*Route 66*--which got
some exposure in the United States. That followed on the heels of
Shellshock Rock, which had been banned at the Cork Film Festival
and gone on, largely on the strength of its having been banned, to cult
film status in the U.S.

More important for this discussion, though, are two
documentaries Davis has made about his home territory of Northern
Ireland. They are both involved with the religious manifestations of
Protestant culture, and are entitled *Dust on the Bible* and *Power in the
Blood.*

Dust on the Bible

When we say that Davis makes documentary films, we're not
really describing adequately what he does. As most documentary film
may be likened to prose writing, so a John T. Davis film is more like
poetry or painting. *Dust on the Bible,* made in 1989, has no real plot
nor narrative structure, yet is quite well tied together. The film
follows a man (never identified) driving across the Irish landscape in
the rain. Intercut with this are scenes of Northern Ireland:
fundamentalist slogans, street-corner preachers, parades. All of this is
set to a measured reading of passages from the Bible (the Book of

Revelations).

The effect, apart from being quite powerful, is of stark contrasts of mood, image, and texture. Once again, the film is an equal balance of emphasis on the verbal, visual, and musical/rhythmic qualities of the piece. Davis explains it this way:

> I don't know what my films are. I don't think of them as documentaries and they're not fiction, but there's drama in them of some description even though they're not acted. . . . I use the film to tell the story.[10]

Power In The Blood

Also shot in 1989, this film too picks up on the theme of religious fundamentalism, but from a different point of view and with a very different form and texture. It also (like *Eat the Peach* and *The Commitments*) accentuates the Irish fascination with American culture--especially as regards popular music and cowboy mythology.

The central figure of *Power in the Blood* is an American country musician named Vernon Oxford. What is unusual about this otherwise unexceptional musician is that he's also a fundamentalist preacher who has made rather frequent trips to Northern Ireland. The film enters Oxford's life in Tennessee, as he's preparing for a trip to Ireland, and follows him throughout that trip as he performs and preaches.

A bit more narrative than *Dust on the Bible*, this film has the advantage of a chronological sequence of events as well as the kind of lyrical visual poetry that makes the other film so appealing to watch. Again utilizing some emotive footage of the various tribal rituals of the political camps in the North to contrast against the dominant story line of Oxford's journey, this makes a very revealing and intimate portrait of the fundamentalist Protestant community. These are Pentecostals, and the scenes of their simple, quiet ways make the shots of violence, drumbeating, and noise of city streets jarring indeed.

The film is sympathetic to Vernon Oxford; there is a simplicity (some might say simplemindedness) to the man which comes across as naively appealing. Davis, however, refrains from implying that Oxford has any answers for Northern Ireland--he just depicts the events, the interaction, between Oxford and the Northern Irish as contrasted with the political/religious conflict going on around them and leaves it for us to absorb.

Certainly, there is a filtration process, an imposition of the filmmaker's viewpoint on a film, no matter how he may refrain from mounting the soapbox to lecture us:

> When you're out shooting a documentary, it's very spontaneous. The process is intellectual, but it's also very emotional at the same time. You're lifting little bits of reality, you're looking for a certain response from a subject. Every frame has got to say something--otherwise it's pointless--and that becomes more and more focused the closer you get to the fine cut of the film. But ultimately, you're using all these images, or at least I am, to say something, however abstract or however direct, about myself and my life and my feelings.[11]

Perhaps the strength of John T. Davis's work derives from its personal nature. Much of the content of his films is intuitive and "organic"; he's proud of the fact that the form of each film grows from the subject itself, and changes as the project progresses. This way of working is something he has in common with O'Sullivan, Comerford, and Black: it may be the thing that defines the "auteur" as distinct from the director, which separates art cinema from commercialism.

Oddly, this quality has not made Davis's talent unmarketable. He has long had a strong affinity for popular culture (particularly rock and country music), and this has gained him entree to the music video market. Such work has included a music video piece for Van Morrison and, in 1993, a documentary about Atlantic Records, *Hip to the Tip.*

Still, though some of the films mentioned in this chapter may go on to some kind of commercial success and exposure outside Ireland, it is safe to say that the primary objective in each of them was personal expression rather than overseas sales, and their focus more regional than international.

Derry Film and Video Workshop: *Hush-A-Bye Baby*

If the Republic of Ireland has been slow to get into the business of filmmaking, Northern Ireland has been even slower. Historically treated as rather a neglected province of Britain, Northern Ireland has been a long time developing its own focus as far as film production is concerned. Although Ulster Television and BBC Northern Ireland have occasionally funded production of film shorts for broadcast, it was not until 1989 that the province had its own film board, the Northern Ireland Film Council. Significant among the beneficiaries of the Film Council was the Derry Film and Video Workshop, founded in 1984, located in Derry City and oriented toward the promotion and production of indigenous film and videotape production of regional interest and focus.

Their first claim to notoriety was a documentary that was funded by Channel Four and then abruptly banned both in Britain and Ireland under their respective political censorship laws. The film was *Mother Ireland,* and its status as a political hot potato came as a bit of a surprise. Far from being a piece of propaganda for either political stance in the North, it is much more a statement of feminist defiance. The film focuses on the marginalization of women in the modern republican movement--dating back to the last century, and features interviews with women who had firsthand experience of that marginalization.

The fact that it was illegal at that time to broadcast interviews with participants in any outlawed organizations involved in the Northern Irish conflict--in Britain and the Republic of Ireland--meant that the film could not be shown on television in either country. The

film was able to be shown theatrically and was widely sold on
videotape. Still, the furor it raised at the time also raised another
question: was it the potential for the expression of outlawed political
ideas that the governments of Britain and the Republic were afraid of,
or was it the threat to male dominance of the political arena?   A
prickly and important question indeed.

    Probably the most prominent work of the Derry Film and Video
Workshop was the feature *Hush-A-Bye Baby,* produced in 1989 and
directed by Margo Harkin. In a simple chronological narrative form,
it tells of a series of significant events in the life of a Derry teenager,
Goretti Friel, and her three girlfriends, Dinky, Majella, and Sinead.
Emer McCourt plays Goretti, and Sinead O'Connor (the singer and
songwriter) plays her friend of the same name.
    The story begins with a fairly broad focus, giving a picture of the
sort of life led by a teenage Catholic girl in the North: unemployed
parents, segregated housing estates, Church schooling, and the
ever-present British military. This film, however, takes its cue from
Pat Murphy's film *Maeve,* following resolutely in its footsteps, and
makes the girls and their concerns the focal issues. Boys, obviously,
figure prominently, as does pregnancy. As the film gradually narrows
its viewpoint to Goretti and her concerns, we see her falling in love
with Ciaran, a boy she meets in after-school Irish class. Inevitably,
they find themselves alone and their sexual attraction takes over. She
discovers she is pregnant, but only after Ciaran has been
"lifted"--arrested on suspicion of terrorist activity.
    Unable to talk to him (he's in prison for an indefinite period of
time, although we're never told if he's been charged) and unable to
confide in her parents, she goes of to the County Donegal Gaeltacht
for summer Irish-language schooling, and to hide her growing belly.
While there, she confides in Dinky, but neither of them knows what to
do. Finally, returned home for the autumn school term, she wakes up
one night screaming and holding her stomach, and there the film
ends, just as her parents open the bedroom door. Presumably,
something has gone wrong, and she's miscarrying, and there we leave

her.

The film, like many films made in the Republic by Harkin's contemporaries, deals quite bluntly with some thorny contradictions in Irish society.   The gulf between the Church and the lives of the young is graphically shown: a priest, lecturing a classroom of girls about the sanctity of marriage, is driven to distraction when they all stare at his crotch and giggle.   Afterward, one of Goretti's friends makes some lewd sexual remarks about him.   In another scene, Ciaran's brother-- lying in the bunk below his--tells an obscene joke about oral sex immediately ʾbefore the film cuts abruptly to a baptism in the church (in which O'Connor sings the hymn).

Notable for its humor and its improbability is a scene in which Goretti and Ciaran are stopped in the street by a British soldier. Asked to spell his name, Ciaran instead rattles off a series of meaningless phrases in Irish, intending to make a mockery of the Brit. Instead, the soldier responds in perfect fluent Gaelic--much better than Ciaran's halting grammar-school speech. This seems to be a gesture of understanding on the part of the filmmaker to those soldiers, who may also be seen as victims of the conflict.

Like *Maeve, Hush-A-Bye Baby* refuses to endorse the violence. In every case, the effects of that violence are shown to be negative. Further, the effects of social segregation and the heavy influence of religion are also shown to be oppressive influences on the people of Northern Ireland: the lack of communication between generations and between church and parishioners, and the negative effects of the divided society on social life and economy are given prominence here, to the exclusion of political issues on either side.   The strife is male-oriented and alien to the people featured in the film; it is as if the women (especially the young ones) are themselves living in segregation from the more violent world of the men which surrounds them. Though they are powerfully affected by it, they are in no way involved in it--theirs is a passive victim's role, and the male-dominated society (including the Church) seems both unable to help and unwilling to try.

Hush-A-Bye Baby was partly funded by Channel Four, and broadcast by it. As such, it was one of the most popular films ever shown on television in Northern Ireland, following on the heels of another film commissioned by Channel Four the previous year, *The Road to God Knows Where*.

Yellow Asylum

Two young graduates of Trinity College, Alan Gilsenan and Martin Mahon, established their company, Yellow Asylum Films, in Dublin for the production of documentary films of Irish interest. Most notable of these was *The Road to God Knows Where*, which traced the movements of young Irish people around Ireland and away from it. Shot in both the Republic and the North, as well as London and New York, it takes a long look at Ireland's youth as disaffected and marginalized, both in their own country and abroad. It is a rather bleak picture of a whole generation disaffected and out of touch with the authority figures in its own country and frequently forced to emigrate elsewhere just to make a decent wage. The film is blunt and depressing, offering neither solution nor hope.

Four years later, they followed with *Between Heaven and Woolworth's*, another documentary. This time, however, the tone was much more upbeat--they simply filmed a number of Ireland's creative luminaries and intercut segments from each. The mix of personalities is critical to the success of the piece: Shane MacGowan (the rock musician), playwrights Tom Murphy and John B. Keane, writer Nuala Ni Dhomhnaill, and filmmaker Neil Jordan. The ways that their ideas about art, creative process, and being Irish intersect make this a revealing and quite uplifting portrait of both the Irish experience and the creative nature without descending into any of the stereotypical imagery which often spoils otherwise well-intentioned documentaries of this sort. Sometimes, the failure of the individual to connect makes the piece quite funny, as is the case with most of the comments made by MacGowan--who seems to live in his own reality quite separate from the rest of the world.

Modest Successes: *Into the West* and *The Secret of Roan Inish*

Some films made for the Irish audience have nonetheless struck a chord outside Ireland and found some unexpected success that way. Two such films, both featuring children and largely aimed at the child audience, have had some measure of success in the mainstream. These are *Into the West* and *The Secret of Roan Inish.*

Featuring Gabriel Byrne (who, though transplanted to Los Angeles, has tried to maintain contact with Irish filmmakers and to generate interest in Irish subjects), *Into the West* is a fairly unexceptional story of a pair of young boys whose destitute lives are salvaged by the entrance of a magical horse.

The featured characters in this film are all travelers, living in roadside encampments or (as are the two boys and their father) in public high-rise housing in Ballymun, near Dublin. The father, John (played by Byrne), makes a few pounds repairing cars in a vacant field. Most of his income seems to be spent on drink, and his two sons Ossie and Tito (Ciaran Fitzgerald and Ruadhri Conroy) spend their time knocking around the city.

There is a lot of footage devoted to the establishment of the tribal nature of the travelers' life, at the end of which the mysterious white horse is introduced by the boys' grandfather. It immediately takes to the younger son, Ossie (Fitzgerald), and he takes it into the flat to live. His brother and father find nothing wrong with this, but their neighbors do, and they and the horse run afoul of the law. The horse is sold, surreptitiously, to a wealthy breeder by one of the police, and begins to win at show jumping contests.

Ossie sees this on TV, and he and his brother go to the next jumping event and steal the horse. They then embark upon a runaway segment which is the predominant reason for the film. Chased west across Ireland (although the scenery looks very much like County Wicklow, which is south of Dublin, not west), they have a number of adventures that are intended to endear them to us and to elaborate upon their feelings of loss in the death of their mother.

Tracked by both police and travelers, they lead a merry chase. Their father has teamed up with a woman "tracker" from his old traveler encampment (played by Ellen Barkin) and together with another traveler (Colm Meaney) they arrive at the seashore before the boys do. Shortly after they're reunited, the Gardai and the wealthy horseman arrive and do battle with them until a senior Garda officer comes along and puts a stop to the violence.

In the fray, Ossie is carried out into the surf on the horse's back, and nearly drowns. He has seen a vision out there, and we now understand that the magic horse was really the spirit of his dead mother. The film ends happily; the horse has vanished, so the baddies go away, and John and the boys go back on the road, acquiescing to their traveler roots.

As a children's film, it spins a good tale. The political significance of a sympathetic portrayal of traveling people would be lost on the non-Irish audience, but that really does the film little harm. It's about children taking matters into their own hands, setting matters right: a theme of universal appeal, well used in children's cinema. The adults are peripheral to the core of the plot, and though they're used to add a specific sort of Irish tone to the piece (and to introduce a bit of old Irish mythology as well), their world is more a background to the kids' world, and subordinate to it.

Similarly structured is *The Secret of Roan Inish*. Though this film rather sneaked into U.S. release, it found a strong audience in mainstream cinemas. Again, the thrust of the film is the idea that children know better than adults.

Set in the northwestern coast, this story also centers upon the lives of two children, and it too features a magical animal. Directed by John Sayles, it tells about a little girl, Fiona (played by Jenni Courtney), who lives with her grandparents--apparently sent there to get her away from the violence of the city.

These grandparents are really island people, transplanted to the mainland by a changing economy and feeling quite out of place there. They are also people with a skeleton in the family closet: involving a (mythical?) half-seal-half-woman called a "silky," it is the family tale of a small boy stolen away by the island seals and floating mysteriously around in his boat-like crib.

Fiona and a friend set out to find the boy, and do so on the island, Roan Inish (literally "seal island"), where her family used to live. Predictably, encroaching economic change (the tourist industry) drives up the rental of the grandparents' house, and the children conspire to restore the ramshackle cottage on the island and convince the family to move back there. They do, of course, and also find the lost boy, resulting in a tearful happy ending.

Like most children's films, this plays up the believability of myth and the happy ending as well as the superior wisdom of the children who are featured. This one also deals with the clash of old culture and new, like *Korea*, but in this case coming down clearly on the side of the old. There is not a great deal about it that is informed by the Irish character; this plot could easily be adapted to another culture and situation. Still, it is clearly set in Ireland and uses Irish talent, and manages to avoid condescension either to the children in the audience or in its depiction of Irish culture.

More important, however, is the success *Roan Inish* found in the U.S. market. Roughly two years after it was made, it reappeared on U.S. screens as a popular children's feature. Perhaps due to its exceptional nature in the context of current trends in children's cinema--it is neither animated nor peopled with warriors from Japanese futurist fantasy--it caught on with American audiences and had quite a long and profitable run, as did *Into the West*. Children's features are not being cranked out by the Los Angeles film factories with quite the speed of adult films, and it may be that this is one area in which Irish talent and subject matter may have an advantage and gain itself further access to mainstream funding and distribution.

Increased Activity

Despite the financial disaster that was *Divine Rapture*, there is a momentum behind the new flurry of film production in Ireland, and it seems to be growing. 1995 saw the release of a half-dozen new films on Irish themes. Shane Connaughton's novel, *The Run of the Country*, has had an international release, although it closed almost as soon as it opened in the United States, and opened to rather bad press in Ireland. Noel Pearson completed *Frankie Starlight*, which had limited distribution in this country, despite featuring Gabriel Byrne and Anne Parillaud (of *La Femme Nikita*). *Circle of Friends* was, of course, something of a hit--reinforcing in some measure the commercial validity of the formula which dictates the insertion of American actors into Irish settings.

Also achieving commercial success, however modest, was *A Man of No Importance*, scripted by Barry Devlin. This was another film which came from his pen in 1994, a year in which Devlin had one feature film in release and two in production. To say that he's a prolific writer is to understate the case. For many years a television writer, advertising copywriter, and TV personality, Devlin began his media career as a musician with the rock band Horslips (who found a latter-day following in the United States and whose recordings can still be found here). His first feature film, shown initially on Irish television and given subsequent theatrical release, was *All Things Bright and Beautiful*, which he wrote and directed. Although aimed at an audience of children and dealing as it does with the simpler pleasures and trials of boyhood, this film makes a wider statement by virtue of its setting in Northern Ireland. Vaguely autobiographical, it centers on a boy (named Barry) growing up in County Tyrone in the relative peacefulness of the 1950s. In this, it shares a place with *December Bride,* taking a close look at the life of a part of the Northern Irish community without focusing on the conflict.

Similarly, Devlin's other feature, *A Man of No Importance,* takes an oblique look at Dublin society of a similar time. The man of the title is Alfie Byrne, a bus conductor with aspirations to high drama and a reverence for the work of Oscar Wilde. As we follow his play-production exploits, we discover that his fascination with Wilde is more than literary: Alfie is homosexual. Once this fact is revealed to us (in a scene in which he puts on a silk bathrobe and styles his hair like Wilde's) the drama focuses upon his need to tell people about himself. This translates to a conflict between Alfie (played by Albert Finney) and the butcher who is his sister's love interest (played by Michael Gambon). Alfie's coming out gets him robbed and beaten, and divides his friends and acquaintances, but represents a sort of triumph. As a social comment, the film shows how little polite Irish society had changed between the Edwardian era when Wilde lived there and the 1960s of this story. The full weight of the righteous churchgoers as well as the official condemnation of both Church and state (in the person of Alfie's boss) is brought to bear, but Alfie stands his ground and is finally rewarded by the loyalty of his theatrical friends. As with many another Irish film, notably Bob Quinn's *Budawanny,* the intolerance of government and Church is shown to be counter to the innate goodness and tolerance of the people themselves.

Following in the path of Jim Sheridan is Dublin theatre director and writer Gerry Stembridge. His first entry into the feature film arena, *Guiltrip,* takes off from the hard realism of many films already discussed here, but without the softening humor of a work like *The Commitments.* More in the vein of *Down the Corner* or *Pigs,* this film looks at the uglier underbelly of modern urban Irish life without sounding a note of mitigating optimism. Though not the sort of imagery preferred by official Ireland, this kind of drama seems to win prizes. *Guiltrip* returned from the Amiens Film Festival with several best-of-category awards, as did Cathal Black's *Korea.*

As Irish filmmakers continue to produce and show films of this
caliber, more new work is under way, indicating a trend toward both a
healthier film community and a greater access to world distribution.
Thaddeus O'Sullivan has completed another feature, *Nothing
Personal,* about the conflict in the North (his first on this subject).
Yet another round of Irish festivals has shown a number of exceptional
shorts and short features, showcasing some fine talent and technical
craftsmanship among the new crop of young filmmakers.

The filmmaking community in Ireland is growing larger and more
productive. There is more funding available through the new Film
Board and the RTE "Short Cuts" program to stimulate the
development of new scripts. Section 35 tax incentives encourage
corporate investment in film projects. There is a sense in Ireland that
the film business is about to take off; the question is, in what
direction?

Notes

1. Roddy Doyle, *Brownbread and War* (London: Secker and
Warburg, 1992).

2. For historical background, I suggest S. J. Connolly's *Religion,
Law, and Power: The making of Protestant Ireland* (Oxford: Oxford
University Press, 1995).

3. Author's interview, 26 June 1994.

4. Author's interview, 27 July 1995.

5. A weekly "city" magazine with events listings, commentary,
and arts reviews.

6. Author's interview, 27 July 1995.

7. Luke Gibbons, "Fragments in Pictures," *Film Base News* 20
(November/December 1990): 8-12.

8. Gibbons, "Fragments in Pictures."

9. Nicky Fennell, "Fanatic Heart," *Film West* 22 (July 1995):
16-18.

10. John O'Regan, *Works 11: John T. Davis* (Kinsale, Ireland: Gandon Editions, 1993): 25.

11. Dermot Lavery, "Power in the Lens," *Film Ireland* (November/December 1992): 21.

CHAPTER NINE
WHAT THESE FILMS MEAN

Mainstreaming

As Rod Stoneman has made clear, the Irish economy is not able to support an indigenous film industry, per se, entirely from within. It is still necessary, for all but the smallest projects, to seek funding from outside the Irish market. This is a situation that is not likely to change in the immediate future, and is the root cause of many of the problems afflicting the film community.

In order to avail of the financial support of those foreign backers whose money is so essential, compromises have had to be made, frequently to the artistic and substantive aspects of a given project. Typically, this may take the form of casting decisions imposed from Britain or California, and the resulting films are those such as *Widows' Peak* and *Circle of Friends*. Hollywood backers, for example, will try to reduce their risk by ensuring that a film shot in Ireland has among its cast a number of names that are "bankable" in the American market, and we can hardly expect otherwise. Such is the nature of that industry.

In the case of a film such as *The Field,* however, what may have been seen as a simple casting compromise to make the film more marketable--the use of Tom Berenger in the role of the foreigner--may have a resonance in the context of the piece which puts a very different complexion upon the whole film, to the point of altering its meaning in a very significant way. The mainstream film industry is a commercial enterprise, and one in which the practice of altering character and story content to bend the piece to the will of its backers or to make it more attractive to a larger segment of the world audience is one of long standing, and thus to be expected.

Artistic integrity, therefore, is inherently a concept alien to the world of commercial cinema. There are innumerable tales of scriptwriters being fired and their work wholly rewritten, or of directors being changed mid-shoot or films being recut after the director's edit. (The proliferation in the video market of "director's cut" reissues of feature films stands in testament to that fact.) This is a problem afflicting any filmmaker, anywhere in the world, who would like to be an auteur but needs financial backing from outside sources to complete the work. In this, the indigenous independent filmmaking community in Ireland is no different from its counterpart in the United States. A Jim Jarmusch, for example, presumably has much the same difficulty with these concerns as does a Cathal Black, and for many of the same reasons.

If anything, the decline of public funding for the arts and humanities which is occurring in the United States may mean that support for filmmaking from the noncommercial sector will be proportionately better in Ireland than here. That would be both ironic and discouraging, but looks as though it may well turn out to be true. As bad as the Irish situation may appear to be, the fact remains that Ireland has a viable Film Board and Arts Council, and a sense that government still has some responsibility to support the arts. While the U.S. government seems to be moving toward the position that the arts should fend for themselves and exist on handouts from the corporate sector, the Irish government seems to be moving toward a position of increased support, however cautiously.

There may be a perception in Ireland that independent filmmakers in the United States have greater financial support than do their Irish counterparts; this is probably untrue. The recent experiences of Robert Rodriguez and Edward Burns would seem to support the contention that independent indigenous film production is as poorly supported in the United States as it is in Ireland, if not more so. That there is more of it is likely attributable to nothing more than a difference of scale: per capita, there may be an even greater level of such activity in Ireland than here.

The simple fact that American independents are located in this country may give them greater access to the eyes and ears of Los Angeles production backers, and thereby ease their way into the commercial mainstream. Of late, it has seemed that success at the Sundance Film Festival is a ticket to recognition by the commercial industry. Certainly their remoteness (both geographically and culturally) from American film circles works against Irish independents in this regard; it is probably an issue to be addressed if the Irish Film Board really intends to promote its indigenous talent into the mainstream market. Cathal Black certainly felt that the Film Board was lacking in experience and ability to assist with placement of *Korea* in the more prominent international festivals:

> There's no follow-through. There's no nourishing. I was close to getting into Berlin, close to getting into Cannes, but they didn't really know how to put their muscle behind it.[1]

The complaint made by Irish independent filmmakers (and certain film critics) about the Irish government's traditional way of managing its film community has been directed at its "film as industry" approach. In this, the government has always assumed that the object was to provide a service industry for an essentially foreign product. Ireland would provide the craftspeople and the physical requisites (studios, locations, hardware) while accepting that the creative impetus would be the purview of the foreign clients.

This seems still to be true, in large measure. That the Film Board could provide substantial backing to *Circle of Friends* or to *Divine Rapture*[2] indicates that the essential conservatism of the government in relation to filmmaking in Ireland has not changed appreciably. It is still necessary for an Irish director to find a measure of success in the foreign market before being regarded as a good risk for funding by the home government. Typically, also, the support provided is only

partial and frequently only script development money--requiring that
the filmmaker find the greater share of the total sum required from
foreign sources, even with Film Board and Section 35 funding. The
consequent effect--whether intended or not--is, therefore, still that the
Irish contribution to feature films made in Ireland remains largely at
the "crafts and trades" level.

To be fair to the present Film Board, it may well take more than a
few years to alter attitudes and policies as long and deeply entrenched
as this. Cathal Black again:

> I think his [Rod Stoneman's] heart is in the right place. He knows
> the contradictions that are there within the Film Board. I think his
> reasoning would be that, if the service industry can be kept going,
> the more nutty fringe might slip through unnoticed and, maybe one
> of these days, cross over.[3]

There is a sense of frustration among the independent filmmakers
who have struggled for several decades to get their films made,
frequently outside the mechanisms of government assistance. All the
rosy predictions surrounding the establishment of the new Film Board
pointed to a new approach on the part of the government, and a new
era in Irish filmmaking. Several years on, these expectations are
proving to have been inflated.

The recent proliferation of film training programs in Irish
colleges has begun to produce a cadre of young filmmakers (or
would-be filmmakers) who are entering the workplace with the
expectation that the growing "industry" will provide for them. This is
putting them in competition with some of the established filmmakers
of Comerford, Quinn, and Black's generation for government support,
and doesn't sit well with those older filmmakers. There is a sense that
the monies are being doled out on a strict rotation basis--as Cathal
Black says, "Joe [Comerford] is worried--and I'm worried too--that we
might be given a certain amount of money, and that's us then: we
have to go back to the end of the queue."[4]

To an extent, that appears to be the way it's being handled. Much
of the funding for noncommercial production is allocated to the

"Short Cuts" program, in which small amounts of money (20,000 to 30,000 punts) are given for short films to be aired on RTE. Normally, these would (for financial reasons) tend to be small-scale and minimally staffed half-hour-long productions. These funds do not (by definition) find their way into feature length productions, fully staffed by crews who are paid a living wage. And while this program may encourage fresh talent and give it a showcase, the issue of support for the production of significant films primarily intended for the Irish audience has still not been addressed in a comprehensive way.

There may be no way out of this dilemma, at least in the near future. Feature-length film production requires sufficiently large amounts of money as to make funding of many such projects from within the Irish economy unlikely. As well as that, the pool of skilled talent required to make films of a high standard of technical quality is probably dependent upon the existence of a "service industry" in support of foreign projects--the development of which has been the goal of a succession of Irish governments since 1958 saw the establishment of Ardmore Studios. In this, we may see a rather delicate balancing act--the need of those who would hope to make a decent living practicing film crafts weighed against the costs that need imposes upon those who would make Irish films to speak to an Irish audience.

Thus far, the practice of granting seed money from the Film Board primarily to encourage further investment from foreign sources has failed to stimulate a quantity of new indigenous production. A given Irish director, not willing to alter a script or cast a film in an inappropriate manner, may thus fail to find adequate funding because of the need to sell the idea to backers outside Ireland.

An alternative, of course, would be for the government to devote larger quantities of money for such indigenous production, but (economic improbability aside) that still wouldn't address problems of distribution and marketing to the home audience. Whether from constraints on distribution dictated by multinational corporate policy (given the near-monopoly Los Angeles has upon film distribution in Europe) or from audience-driven market considerations, it is also true that the films made by Irish independents for the Irish are not given much exposure to their intended audience.

Like much of the rest of the world, Ireland has been invaded by the mass-market multiplex cinemas, and the fare presented therein is precisely the same as that which is shown to American and British audiences.   An unfortunate effect of the liberalization of film censorship in Ireland has been an increased public appetite for the relatively vacuous, violent, and superfluous commercial product that Hollywood routinely turns out, and that largely ignores issues of substance, especially in the Irish context.

In this respect, the attempts by earlier Irish governments to protect the sensibility of the Irish people from outside influence may have had some beneficial side effects. Unfortunately, the concurrent restraint on indigenous expression and the fundamentally capitalistic nature of Ireland's subsequent entry into the mainstream, when it finally came, mitigated against the wholehearted embrace by government of the arts, and of film as an art form.

Thus it remains unlikely that further attempts by Irish filmmakers to speak to the home audience will find the way much easier than did their predecessors in the recent past.   In fact, the success of foreign-produced commercial films shot in Ireland (but using it as little more than a scenic backdrop) seems to bolster the film-as-industry brief and may serve to siphon money and native talent away from home-produced projects.

No doubt independent Irish filmmakers will continue, at whatever rate they can manage, to express themselves on subjects of importance to the Irish psyche. Some of these, whether in art-house cinemas at home or in other countries, on television, or (much more rarely) in mainstream cinema, will find audiences and resources enough to support themselves. To some, this will never be satisfactory. A final comment on this from Cathal Black:

> There's no use having the film board, having RTE with a mandate
> for independent filmmaking, Section 35, and you can't make a living
> in your own country as a filmmaker. There's no point. We've all

been seduced by the notion that you accept all this. The only one who is saying, "I'm a filmmaker and I deserve to work in my own country" is Joe Comerford.[5]

Thus it still is that, on both Irish and international screens, "Irish" films are almost exclusively shot by foreign production companies or adapted heavily to suit the international market. Not only is it difficult for people outside Ireland to see the work of indigenous Irish writers and directors, it is nearly as difficult for those living in Ireland. It is in this context that we should evaluate those films that do make it onto any screen, anywhere.

They are, as we have seen, few and far between. They are also the product of exceptional tenacity, determination, and singleness of purpose: the sheer difficulty of finding the resources to make them necessarily ensures that. Equally, they tend to be possessed of a singular clarity of vision. (By this I don't necessarily mean that each makes a clear and simple statement, but rather that the makers must have a firm grasp of their concept for the finished product--and a near-obsessive desire to realize it--in order to see each project through to completion.)

15. Product of tenacity: Bob Quinn's *Poitín.* (Courtesy of the Irish Film Archive and Bob Quinn)

Unfortunately, that is often where the process stops, and this is an area in which effort could be made: to acquire screen time and broaden exposure. Certainly, the Irish Film Centre is a step in the right direction, although it is only one such cinema, and is regarded among Dubliners as an art-house venue. There are others around Ireland, but they are few and their existence threatened. The Claddagh Palace in Galway (home of the Galway Film Fleadh) is one, and rumors are that it is to be demolished to make way for an apartment block--another old cinema falling victim to a multiplex.

Outside Ireland, there are some hopeful signs. London has always had its share of independent cinemas, and the work of Irish directors has turned up there on occasion. (I first saw *Reefer and the Model* at the Metro Cinema in Soho.) The recent retrospective season of indigenous Irish films sponsored by the Film Society of Lincoln Center, in New York, threw an unusual amount of attention on the subject and on these works while underlining the rarity of such an occurrence and the scarcity of prints. There seems to be a resurgence of interest in Irish culture among the American population, and other film festivals here are screening Irish work. Still, it's a long way from mass-market exposure, and the nature of the world market is likely to keep it that way.

To Whom Are They Speaking?

I mentioned in the first chapter the great diversity of expression coming from such a geographically small island; thus it is that there is no one answer to the above question. If you ask six Irish people what the Irish think about a given issue, you'll likely get six answers. This may be taken to be a sign of a depth of thought and consideration and a healthy respect for the subtle shadings of ideas, as well as an indication of the complexity and confusion underlying Irish history and politics.

In its simplest form, then, it seems that there are two general groups within which Irish filmmaking talent may be categorized. These are, on the one hand, the people who got into the craft before it became a subject taught in art college, and, on the other, those who've studied in those colleges since. This is a generational separation, but it is more than that.

The established, older voices in the independent community generally belong to those who had to scrape together resources and fight to get their films made, to get equipment and crews, to learn about the medium. Leading examples would be Bob Quinn and Cathal Black; both have largely developed their styles of expression independently, and have as their fundamental motivation a sense of personal mission. They are powerful individualists, as are many of their contemporaries.

The newer voices have come into the field largely since the perception of a growing film industry was popularized, and many of them have done so with the expectation (and primary objective) that they will earn a decent living thereby. There are notable exceptions: John Moore and Alison Toomey, among others, have made films that are strong personal expressions and may not have commercial potential at their core. Others, however, seem quite happy to leap on the bandwagon of foreign-produced commercial product if that will pay them a living wage. This is a matter of concern to some of those older directors, and the hope seems to be that some of the younger talent will find its own voice despite, to some extent, embracing the commercial industry. The work of John T. Davis and Thaddeus O'Sullivan would seem to indicate that such a compromise is possible.

Neil Jordan has consistently maintained that he has tried to be true to his desire to tell Irish stories and address Irish issues, while remaining in the commercial network. It would be quite a feat if one were to do so without any compromises; given that, both he and Jim Sheridan seem to have succeeded to a remarkable degree.

That said, the films that do get produced in Ireland by Irish filmmakers tend to address the Irish audience as a first priority. That is as it ought to be, however it may mitigate against some of those projects being produced at all. It is a measure of the sense of urgency felt by that segment of the Irish population that they've been spurred to do what they had to do to speak to certain issues. As a country still emerging from its isolationist past, and one for which both the Civil War and the Partition of the North (the issue over which that war was fought) remain largely unresolved, the process of self-definition is both a contentious and an emotive one. It is also essential to the health of the nation, and to any effort to move forward in other areas of concern. Comerford has quite clear ideas about the role of films in this process:

> There never was a greater need for art in order to be informed
> personally and publicly about what's happening in our society and
> what's happening to us personally. There never was a greater need
> for it for our survival. That's the context in which I'm talking about
> art, yet at the same time there was never (in my experience) a
> greater resistance to art.[6]

While such views would be those we'd expect from a filmmaker who is considered both radical and contentious, it should be taken as significant that Neil Jordan (in some minds symbolic of the compromise with commercialism) reiterates them. In a recent benefit showing of *The Crying Game*, reported in *Film Ireland* (August/September 1995), Jordan made the following comments:

> Marginal voices are being excluded by a subtle interplay of the
> culture of approval and the culture of the commercial marketplace
> itself. I think creative voices end up not knowing where they are. . .
> It strikes me that one could imagine a conspiracy of forces at work at
> the moment, to build a picture of contemporary Ireland that is safe,
> modern, very European, and more specifically, middle class,
> embarrassed about certain aspects of its past.

Jordan sums up well. Having emerged from a past characterized by an agrarian economy and a heavy-handed enforcement of isolationist policy, built upon an idyllic mythos of a self-sufficient Gaelic Catholic culture into a wholehearted embrace of Western capitalism and the values of the industrialized middle class, it is small wonder that many Irish heads were spinning. After several centuries of fairly static character as regards significant political change, the twentieth has been, for Ireland, a most remarkable and confused one.

Having begun this century as yet another colony of the British Empire, the Irish saw--after a fierce and bloody guerrilla war that spared few--the dissolution of their formal subjugation to that Empire. Immediately upon the achievement of independence, the twenty-six county Republic went to war with itself over the issue of Partition. When the Civil War ended, there was no clear victory and no formal resolution: many of the die-hards were killed by their own government and many others fled the country. Thus, the IRA was both an outlaw organization and a figure of mythical heroism, depending upon the occasion and the speaker. Throughout the 1930s, 40s, and 50s, these issues were not dealt with publicly; the hand of government saw to that, and took upon itself the task of the definition of Irishness, to the exclusion of dissenting voices.

Thus, when the country threw itself abruptly into mainstream economy, its populus was also abruptly drawn into mainstream culture and aspirations. Beginning in the late 1950s, pop culture from America and Britain was embraced by the young people of Ireland concurrent with the gradual move up the economic ladder toward middle-class status and away from an agricultural economic base. Add to this the socialization of medical care and the infusion of resources into education, and the full entry of Ireland into mainstream Euro-American culture seems (with hindsight) inevitable.

In the process of changing directions, however, the country has overlooked some aspects of itself. Where the "Gaelic" model was imposed by de Valera and his Fianna Fail government to cover the scars of civil war and redirect the nation's energy, a new myth was constructed by that government's successors to make the Irish themselves more marketable to the world. Some of this has been done by the tourist industry, and some by those charged with the task of enticing foreign business into the country. In either case, those aspects of the Irish character which did not suit the purpose have been overlooked, and it is this to which Neil Jordan and Joe Comerford both refer.

Historically, Ireland has typically been on the fringes of world culture and a pawn in other countries' power struggles. It was ignored by the Romans and treated as a disposable quantity by the French, when Wolfe Tone tried to organize an invasion to remove the British in the late eighteenth century. In the present century, it has been largely overshadowed by British culture next door and American culture across the Atlantic. Its lack of access to world media has virtually ensured, until very recently, that the definition of Irish culture--not only to the world, but to itself--has been substantially ceded to foreigners. Lack of economic clout, military strength, and size have all contributed to the assumption on the part of larger and more powerful nations that they have the right to characterize the nature of Irish culture.

Not surprisingly, many Irish people have taken offense at this. The incursion of foreign images of themselves into their own cinemas and television programs is often offensive, in addition to being misrepresentative. No less than American Indians or Italians, they resent being characterized as the two-dimensional "bad guys" in mindless Hollywood adventure films like *Patriot Games*. Equally, they have come to resent being portrayed as the argumentative/devious/alcoholic bumpkins of so many British films made over the last several decades.

What rankles most, however, is not that the world outside Ireland is fed these images, but the fact that these are also the images they see on screen at home. It is, in part, the frustration at being misrepresented by foreigners in films shot in Ireland and then shown there that drives many of the "fringe" filmmakers to produce. Their voices, however muted by the lack of muscle required to force them into world consciousness, are eager to be heard, to counter the fictions about Ireland being dished up in Los Angeles and elsewhere.

Perhaps the strongest statement on this subject is that made by the simple fact that these films are being shot at all. The need to take part in one's own cultural definition is powerful, but especially so in

Ireland, and especially at this juncture. The combination of a turbulent recent history and a long prior history of repressive government with the recent release of much of that repressive force has created a relatively unrestricted forum for discussion and a ready-made set of burning issues. It is, in all likelihood, no accident that the artistic climate in Ireland--film, literature, theater, music--is so highly charged and productive. There is a pressing need to be met. For the first time in centuries, the restrictions to self-expression are coming off, and people with the requisite talents are moving to take advantage of that.

It is a measure of the importance of this process that those who are making "dangerous" films are willing to make the sacrifices necessary to complete them. It is a measure of the importance of this process to the larger Irish society that these films are subjected to such close scrutiny and, sometimes, harsh criticism. There is a growing sense of empowerment in the society as a whole that makes people conscious of the significance of these events to their society's future. However uneven and ill conceived the path to capitalism may have been, however difficult the relationship between government and its filmmakers and other artists, change has taken place and promises to continue.

The goal of industrialization has largely been achieved, as has the goal of a largely middle-class society, whatever one may think of their merits. Despite the statistics that seem to Americans to portray a high unemployment rate (the Irish government appears to calculate these figures differently than does the U.S. government), the reality is that today's Ireland is no longer a nation of stagnant rural poverty, but one of largely urban upwardly mobile comparative prosperity. They are better educated than most Americans, have aspirations much like ours, and (though emigration is still the ticket to upward mobility for some) better prospects for the realization of those aspirations in their own country than was the case thirty years ago.

Thus, when Joe Comerford claims that he has the right to expect to make films in his own country, and Cathal Black reiterates that, or when Pat Murphy laments the relegation of Ireland to a quaint scenic background for silly Hollywood fictions, they are all laying claim to the right to speak to their own people. Their efforts to exercise this right have been hindered or obstructed in many cases and many ways, as Neil Jordan says, by a "conspiracy of forces": political, ideological, economic. Still, not only because many of us are their cousins or because Irish culture has had a profound impact on American and European culture, but because *they* have been observing *us* these many years and have some valuable insights to offer, we too may find the work of these indigenous Irish filmmakers enlightening.

The Issues: Speaking to the Irish Audience

From the sampling of films in preceding chapters, we've seen some of the issues that are the stuff of choice for Irish independents. The documentary work done over the last several decades has done much to record facts of history and culture that may have gone unrecorded or been distorted by myth and legend. The dramas have tended to address issues of historic or social importance that are perceived to have been glossed over or otherwise misrepresented. Whatever the chosen form, there is a common thread through much of this work: the need to address an omission or to reexamine an accepted issue in a new light.

The documentaries range from David Shaw-Smith's meticulous preservation of dying aspects of Irish culture to John T. Davis's lyrical poem-documentaries dealing more with states of mind than facts. Somewhere between is a film like Bob Quinn's *Atlantean,* which supports the contention (not without its basis in evidence) that the Irish owe their ancestry to the Arabs of North Africa as much as the Aryans of northern Europe. There is, throughout much of this work, a desire to debunk myths, whether they be those of the origins of Irish culture, of the lack of a sophisticated indigenous culture or artistry in

Ireland, or of the idea that the conflict in the North is a simple clash of religious beliefs. We find, as befits a renaissance, a need to reexamine the body of accepted knowledge in order to move on. In this context, *Man of Aran* becomes little more than a quaint museum piece--a foreigner's view of an Irish culture that certainly does not exist now if, in fact, it ever did.

There is also a distinctly Irish way of making a film, which, as Jim Sheridan believes, has its origins in the oral tradition of the old culture. Though it relies heavily on dialogue to carry the story along, it is not the relatively simplistic expository dialogue which so often clutters Hollywood's commercial cinema.

What becomes important in much indigenous Irish film--as, indeed, in its stage drama--is the meter and inflection of its delivery. The words often have a tonal/textural quality which makes use of the verbal to color a scene as much as to convey information. This is taken to a very effective extreme in *Dust on the Bible,* in which the sense of the words takes a back seat to the interplay of their poetic quality with rhythm, color, and texture. When it works well, the technique is magical, as in *December Bride* or *Budawanny,* in which the director cooks up a very potent brew of all the above, combined with a strong and compelling story.

As Sheridan also noted, the Irish have long used language as a sort of weapon, as a means of self-defense. Thus, meanings can have many shades, and one needs to hear many things spoken aloud in order to divine their real intent. It is often difficult in Gaelic or in Irish-English to discern the shades of meaning from the written text, and in this the storytelling tradition lives on. Thus, a work like *Finnegan's Wake* may look so dense as to be inaccessible on the page, but takes on a kind of music when spoken aloud (as in a television presentation done some years ago for RTE).

With this tradition behind them, Irish filmmakers are positioned well to take on their medium and to stretch and expand it in some new and exciting ways. Many are finding that they have a quite highly developed and equally subtle visual sense which combines powerfully with an appreciation for the verbal and a wry wit--all of which really do abound in Ireland. (Anyone desiring evidence of this should take a look at John Moore's short *He Shoots, He Scores.*)

16. An Irish view of a postapocalyptic future: James Mahon gets worried in John Moore's short, *He Shoots, He Scores.* (Courtesy of Clingfilms Ltd.)

The storytelling tradition is also a personal one; it evolved long before the idea of addressing mass audiences had entered anyone's head, and this approach too has carried over. Far from handicapping Irish filmmakers, the ability to make films which seem to address their audiences as though they were a small gathering may well work to their favor. The emotive impact of *My Left Foot* and *In the Name of the Father* owe much to this ability. Contrasted to the current Hollywood formula--substituting heavily post-produced action sequences for emotional and intellectual engagement--this kind of filmmaking is quite a refreshing change. The success of these films in the world market would indicate that there are a number of people who are ready for such a change.

Part of the personalized approach to filmmaking may be derived from another function of the storytelling tradition--the use of a subject's evolution through successive retellings as a means of understanding and self-definition. In mainstream films, the tendency is toward a declamatory stance: the filmmaker defining and stating the "truth." In the context of indigenous Irish film, much of the work serves rather as an exploratory tool for the culture as a whole to use in the process of addressing and understanding issues of common importance. Joe Comerford clearly views this as one of his motivations, in this instance as regards *High Boot Benny*:

> Obviously, it's a huge propaganda requirement to give an impression of what's happening in the North. I cannot sit here and say I know what's going on in the North; I don't, but in *High Boot Benny* what I was trying to do was, at first hand, try and understand what's going on in the North--to get out of denial and understand what is happening.[7]

Although Ireland--and the rest of the world--is unlikely to think of itself as Third World, it is certainly an emergent culture, like many another former colony of the British Empire. (It is worth noting, however, a quip made by Jimmy Rabbitte, Jr., in *The Commitments*, in reply to a grim civil servant in the dole office who berates him for failing to find work: "Sure, we're a Third World country--what can you do?") As an emergent culture, and a fairly homogeneous one, Ireland has a common group memory upon which anyone attempting to speak to the group can draw with assurance. In that respect, it resembles much of the cinema of the Third World, and it is this common ground connecting the individual members of the audience which permits the use of the cinema as an exploratory device rather than a medium of simple statement.[8]

Thus, a film like *Korea* can assume a foreknowledge of the events of the Civil War as well as the impact those events had on Ireland's emotions and its subsequent political life and structure. The intensity of the Civil War in the emotive landscape also assures a high level of personal engagement from an Irish audience, which would not be expected from a foreign one. This is well demonstrated in the case of Neil Jordan's *The Crying Game*. This film found a huge success in the American market, despite having attracted little attention in Briatin and some harsh criticism in Ireland. The collective understanding of the problem of the North would assure an engagement by an Irish audience whose need to understand that situation would draw them into the film, even if they found they disagreed with its message. The British audience, having a different shared experience, would not automatically engage with it, and their reaction would be as to a messy foreign conflict that is not as significant a factor in their lives and with which they might prefer not to deal. The American audience, however, was drawn to the film because of the issue of sexual identity (and the titillation associated therewith) revolving around the character Dil and her/his relationship with Fergus--an issue that was largely marginal to the Irish audience. In effect, then, the Irish and the American audiences may be said to have seen two entirely different films, despite having viewed the same one.

This is a problem in a film such as *High Boot Benny* or *Korea*. The extent to which the shared experience--the group memory--of the primary audience is relied upon is the extent to which it will be difficult for an audience outside that group to engage with the primary issues of the film. In the context of the need to understand the nuances of the Northern conflict, *High Boot Benny* is a subtle piece, probing the situation on many levels. To those without that collective experience behind them, the need to explore those nuances and use them in a personal or social quest for understanding is diminished or eliminated, and the film seems obscure and puzzling.

To an audience accustomed to film as statement, to film as diversion and as a medium of nonspecific "event" rather than a component part of an ongoing dialogue, such a work is either without meaning or interesting for other reasons than those intended by its maker. This is a problem for an indigenous filmmaker in an emergent culture on the fringe of Europe (itself a fringe culture in the context of mainstream cinema).

It has certainly been a problem for Neil Jordan and for Jim Sheridan, although both seem to have been able, in certain instances, to do the required balancing act and provide sufficient interest for both the Irish and the world audiences. It is an indication of their desire to lay claim to the title of "Irish filmmaker," as opposed to a filmmaker *from* Ireland, that each has returned to probe those issues of particular political and emotional sensitivity to the Irish collective conscience and thus engage in the cultural dialogue. As a Southerner, Jordan has returned to the issue of the North, and has now engaged in an examination of the War of Independence and the Civil War in his film about Michael Collins. (Collins' life is the stuff of Irish legend: he was the strategist who drove British military rule out of Ireland, and also, in some minds, the victim of a suspicious and politically opportune death.) Contentiousness notwithstanding, much of Jordan's work does amount to a dialogue with the Irish psyche and puts him, in that sense, on a plane with Quinn, Comerford, et al.

Speaking to the European Audience

Speaking to Europe and Britain, the indigenous Irish film community seems to be both reaching out for inclusion in the European community and asserting its individuality. In a very tangible way, contact with Europe is beneficial: as we've seen, much of the funding for film projects with Irish themes has come from other European Union countries, especially France and Germany. As Europe forges its own identity, interest in cross-cultural exchange between member nations may be on the rise. Also, as Europe takes responsibility for support of the arts, funding for film production (especially noncommercial projects) within member countries increases. There are several such funds at work, and indigenous Irish film production has already benefited from them.

Economically, it is important for Ireland to be seen to be a European nation. It is marketing itself to multinational corporations as a manufacturing and distribution point for the entire European market, and the more outward signs of its inclusion in the greater

European economy and culture it can show, the greater its credibility in this effort. To the extent that elements of Irish culture earn a place in the popular culture of Europe, Ireland may be seen to be a player in the European economy.

Historically, however, Ireland's failure to deal with its filmmakers outside the context of industry has mirrored the predominant approach taken by Euro-government. Both the European Union and the Council of Europe have established funding bodies for the promotion of film production, and predictions have been made of the establishment of a European answer to Hollywood. In effect, this amounts to a vision of a giant version of Ardmore Studios--a "Hollywood on the Seine"--and is unrealistic both because it takes a purely industrial view of the medium, and because it presupposes a cultural homogeneity that does not exist in Europe.[9] While certain independent filmmakers in Ireland have benefited from these grant programs, it is hard to see how a centralized film production industry on the continent would be particularly useful to them.

Cathal Black has given us an apt description of the kind of project which can result from a program that overlooks differences of cultural identity, regionalism, and aesthetics (known in European film circles as a "Europudding"):

> There's a script I read which started as a Swedish novel adapted by an American guy which was obviously meant to be shot in America and is owned by a German company who shook hands with a company here and have never produced a feature drama in their lives. It'll be directed by an Englishman . . .[10]

Equally, there is a strong desire to take control of the perception of the Irish in Britain. This may prove more difficult, since the denigration of Irish culture is so deeply embedded in British tradition that those practicing it may not even be aware of what they're doing. As Terry George observed[11], a film made in Ireland by an Irish director is typically only acknowledged as an Irish film by the British press if it is a financial failure. Thus, *The Field* was reported in Britain as an Irish film, while *My Left Foot* had been embraced as British.

As a means of discourse, films made for the Irish population may find in Britain an emigrant population which has arrived recently enough or retained enough of its shared memory to respond as would a native Irish one. Because the Irish emigrant population in Britain is so close to its home country, and because of the nature of the emigrant communities there, these people may be better attuned to the subtexts and background assumptions inherent in much indigenous Irish cinema than are their counterparts in the United States.

Speaking to the World

I've noted that most of the work of indigenous independent Irish filmmakers has been shown (*when* it has been shown) in the United States and the world outside Europe on the screens of art-house cinemas. It is unlikely that this pattern will change anytime soon.

In much that has been written about alternative cinema, whether in the context of Europe or in the context of the Third World, the point has been made that there is a distinction to be drawn between Hollywood and the United States. It would be as incorrect to conclude that Hollywood film product is reflective of the reality of life and aspiration in the U.S. as it would be to conclude that Hollywood's portrayal of Irish culture is also an accurate one. The rivalry between Los Angeles and New York as filmmaking centers, for instance, is as much a cultural one as an industrial one: it is an open secret that film and television product emanating from Hollywood studios and purporting to be "about" other parts of the U.S. is often laughably inaccurate. The existence of longtime Eastern holdouts against "Los Angelesation" (Kevin Rockett's word) such as Woody Allen, Martin Scorsese, and Barry Levinson stands as proof of this.

In fact, the Los Angeles industry, often inappropriately referred to as "the American film industry," is more a multinational entity than a national one. It feeds upon a worldwide talent pool and directs its product toward the largest audience possible--regardless of national, cultural, or language barriers. It seems likely that the bland uniformity of style and form to which much of this work is held may be tied to the industry's need to cater for so many different tastes. Certainly, the preponderance of fantasy variations upon the structure of the Western (*Star Wars*) or the classic detective story (*Blade Runner*) fits neatly into this supposition: as export product, it is superbly marketable worldwide.

Much of European cinema, by contrast, is regional. Because of language differences, cultural conflicts, and memories of conflicts of more violent sorts, borders are still important in Europe. Because of the history of misunderstanding and violent conflict (which, despite the cease-fire in effect as I write this, is still a very real threat and vivid memory) between the British and Irish, the physical closeness of the two countries is not matched by an innate understanding of each other's cultures--in spite of the "shared" language.

The process of self-definition or reinvention is one of reaction to an image imposed from elsewhere. In the early history of the Free State and Republic, it came from Irish government; before that, it came from London or from Dublin Castle--the seat of British government in Ireland. Thus it may be perfectly logical that the Irish, of all the Europeans, should be the most likely to turn to American culture both to find models from which to borrow and to advertise their reentry into world consciousness.

The fruit of such reinvention is recognition, and a number of Irish artists have achieved that in the United States. Particularly in terms of popular music, Irish bands have enjoyed an entree to a U.S. audience perhaps larger than other Europeans. Irish traditional music still enjoys a strong popularity in this country, and Ireland's pop music--informed as it is by traditional forms--has always found a ready access to cult status as well as the occasional starring role. Musicians such as U2, Sinead O'Connor, Van Morrison, The Pogues, The Cranberries, and Clannad have sent a clear message to the younger audience of Americans: the young Irish are clever, sophisticated, literate, and set to carve a place for themselves in world culture.

Lately, some young Irish writers are beginning to follow this lead. Eoin Macnamee, following in the footsteps of Patrick McCabe, Roddy Doyle, and Shane Connaughton, is finding an audience here. Presumably, when the film of his novel *The Last of the High Kings* is released, Ferdia MacAnna will also join those ranks.

Paddy Breathnach, when commenting upon his film *Ailsa,* stated that his intention was to make a film that was informed by Germanic style--a plain attempt to reach out to another culture. As a gesture of inclusion in the new Europe it has some significance; as a gesture of release from isolationist politics, however, it has a more powerful impact. Much of the need for Irish filmmakers to get their work seen in Europe and the United States is (access to funding aside) rooted in the need for the world to see them acting in their own behalf. For too long, their position in the world, their position within their own culture, was dictated to them and articulated for them by others. In this light, the films being made by indigenous Irish directors are part of a dialogue with the world as well as with their own people. It matters to them what their American cousins think of them--as with their British ones--but it matters much more that they are finally able to speak for themselves on issues of importance to themselves, and the exercise of this ability in itself is meaningful.

If, in the process of doing so, they introduce a different style of filmmaking/storytelling--perhaps a more complex, layered style with more reliance on subtlety and wordplay than postproduction--might some of us not find that refreshing and interesting? Just as new Irish music has come to shape world taste (and occasionally to dominate, as it did with U2), so might Irish filmmaking.

It may seem frustrating to those laboring away on the fringes of the Irish film "industry" that so few of their films seem to break into world consciousness, or even into multiplex cinemas at home. Still, it must be remembered that, twenty years ago, none were breaking through. It must also be remembered that those who did make the break and get mainstream distribution began on those same fringes.

It is often an accident that a particular individual film strikes a chord with a producer or distributor, wins a prize in a film festival, or in some other way makes the transition from regional to multinational success. Frequently, there are many equally good films that don't make the leap, and for no apparent reason other than chance. It is those of us among the potential audience who are at the mercy of the commercial production and distribution system who are the losers in this. Combing the art-house cinemas sometimes produces satisfactory results, as does searching out scarce videotape copies or scanning the listings of "art-house television" channels.

At present, there is little organization in the distribution of art cinema releases. Prints may be hard to find, and it may be all but impossible to find information about new work by independent filmmakers in other countries so as to know what films to look for. Cable television, by virtue of its voracious appetite for new things to show, tends to help with this, and overseas film publications can be quite helpful in the identification of new works and filmmakers. Still, unless one lives in or near a large city, the likelihood of finding an art-house cinema in which to see these films as their makers intended is slim indeed.

Those who are sufficiently interested and fortunate to travel abroad with any regularity may be able to search out indigenous films in Ireland. Ideally, of course, attendance at one of the film festivals which abound in Ireland is the best way to see the newest work. Still, there are film festivals in the United States which would book these films if they knew there was a demand; despite their concern about preservation, the staff of the Irish Film Archives take their mission--the dissemination of the body of work--very seriously indeed and do whatever they can to get such work shown in as many places as possible. The renewed interest in Irish culture in the United States also means that there are more and livelier venues for the exhibition of Irish films. Thus it is that, outside the mechanisms of a strictly commercial Los Angeles-based industry, there are growing opportunities for indigenous Irish filmmakers' work to be shown in this country.

If the structure of these events grows to accommodate popular interest, then a suitable route of access may emerge to the greater audience. If *Dancing at Lughnasa* can make money on Broadway and *The Secret of Roan Inish* become a success in American mainstream cinemas, then it may well be nothing more than a matter of finding opportunity for exposure which will make the difference for many other works.

There is little about *Korea* or *High Boot Benny* or *Power in the Blood* that is substantially more difficult for a non-Irish audience to grasp than there was in *My Left Foot* or *The Commitments*. Still, the perception by those who are the gatekeepers of the multinational distribution network seems to be that there might be, with the result that some very fine examples of cinematic expression have been kept from an audience who might well appreciate them.

Notes

1. Author's interview.
2. An American film, featuring Marlon Brando, which went bankrupt during shooting in Ireland in August 1995.
3. Author's interview, 27 July 1995.
4. Author's interview.
5. Author's interview.
6. Author's interview, 26 June 1994.
7. Author's interview.
8. See *Questions of Third Cinema*, Jim Pines and Paul Willemen, eds. (London: British Film Institute, 1989).
9. See Paul Hainsworth, "Politics, Culture, and Cinema in the New Europe" in *Border Crossing: Film in Ireland, Britain, and Europe*, John Hill, Martin McLoone, and Paul Hainsworth, eds (Belfast/London: Institute of Irish Studies/British Film Institute, 1994): 8-33.
10. Author's interview.
11. Comments made during a panel discussion at the Walter Reade Theatre, New York, 26 June 1994.

SELECTED BIBLIOGRAPHY

Carty, Ciaran. *Confessions of a Sewer Rat: A Personal History of Censorship and the Irish Cinema.* Dublin: New Island Books, 1995.

Connaughton, Shane, and Jim Sheridan. *My Left Foot.* London: Faber and Faber, 1989.

Hill, John, Martin McLoone, and Paul Hainsworth. *Border Crossing: Film in Ireland, Britain, and Europe.* Belfast/London: Institute for Irish Studies/British Film Institute, 1994.

Jordan, Neil. *Angel.* London: Faber and Faber, 1989.

------. *The Crying Game.* London: Vintage, 1993.

------. *Night in Tunisia.* London: Vintage, 1993.

------. *High Spirits.* London: Faber and Faber, 1989.

Jordan, Neil, and David Leland. *Mona Lisa.* London: Faber and Faber, 1986.

McIlroy, Brian. *Irish Cinema: An Illustrated History.* Dublin: Anna Livia Press, 1988.

O'Regan, John. *Works 11: John T. Davis.* Kinsale, Ireland: Gandon Editions, 1993.

O'Toole, Fintan. *The Politics of Magic: The Work and Times of Tom Murphy.* Dublin: Raven Arts Press, 1987.

Rockett, Kevin. *The Irish Filmography.* Dublin: Red Mountain Press, 1996.

Rockett, Kevin, and Eugene Finn. *Still Irish: A Century of the Irish in Film.* Dublin: Red Mountain Press, 1995.

Rockett, Kevin, Luke Gibbons, and John Hill. *Cinema and Ireland.* London: Routledge, 1987.

SELECTED FILMS

Cathal Black
Korea (1995)
Our Boys (1981)
Pigs (1984)

Brendan Bourke
Fishing the Sloe-Black River (1995)

Paddy Breathnach
Ailsa (1994)
The Long Way Home (1995)

Joe Comerford
Down the Corner (1978)
High Boot Benny (1994)*
Reefer and the Model (1988)*
Traveller (1978)
Withdrawal (1974)

Shane Connaughton (writer)
My Left Foot (1989)+
The Playboys (1992)+
The Run of the Country (1995)

John T. Davis
Between the Line (1977)
Dust on the Bible (1989)
Heart on the Line (1990)
Hip to the Tip (1993)
Hobo (1991)

Power in the Blood (1989)
Protex Hurrah (1980)
Route 66 (1985)
Self-Conscious Over You (1981)
Shellshock Rock (1978)
Transfer (1975)
The Uncle Jack (1995)

Barry Devlin
All Things Bright and Beautiful (1994)
A Man of No Importance (1995)+

Roddy Doyle (Writer)
The Commitments (1991)+
Family (1994)
The Snapper (1993)+
The Van (1995)

Paul Duane
Misteach Baile Atha Cliath (1995)

Alan Gilsenan (Yellow Asylum)
Between Heaven and Woolworth's (1992)
The Road to God Knows Where (1988)

Margo Harkin
Hush-a-bye Baby (1989)*
Mother Ireland (1988)*

Kieran Hickey
Attracta (1983)
Criminal Conversation (1980)
Exposure (1978)

Neil Jordan
Angel (1982)+
The Company of Wolves (1984)+
The Crying Game (1992)+
High Spirits (1988)+
Interview With the Vampire (1994)+
Michael Collins (1996)
The Miracle (1991)+

Mona Lisa (1986)+

Mark Kilroy

Hard Shoulder (1989)

Diarmuid Lawrence

The Hanging Gale (1995)*

Loving (1995)

Tom McArdle

It's Handy When People Don't Die (1980)

The Kinkisha (1977)

Mary McGuckian

Words Upon the Windowpane (1995)

John Moore

He Shoots, He Scores (1995)

Pat Murphy

Anne Devlin (1984)

Maeve (1981)

Maurice O'Callaghan

Broken Harvest (1994)

Pat O'Connor

The Ballroom of Romance (1982)*

Cal (1984)+

Circle of Friends (1995)+

Peter Ormrod

Caught in a Free State (1983)

Eat the Peach (1986)+

Thaddeus O'Sullivan

December Bride (1990)+

*Fanatic Hearts [*a.k.a.* Nothing Personal] (1995)*

The Woman Who Married Clark Gable (1985)

Bob Quinn

Atlantean (1984)

The Bishop's Story (1994)

Budawanny (1987)

Caoineadh Airt Ui Laoire (1975)

Poitin (1978)

Jim Sheridan
  The Field (1990)+
  In the Name of the Father (1993)+
  My Left Foot (1989)+
Gerry Stembridge
  Guiltrip (1995)
Fergus Tighe
  Clash of the Ash (1987)
Alison Toomey
  Where the Heart Remains (1995)
Orla Walsh
  Bent Out of Shape (1995)

* Available on PAL videotape (European standard).
+ Available also on NTSC videotape (North American standard).

INDEX

A

B

C

E

Eat the Peach, 150-154, 175
Edwards, Hilton, 6
Emmett, Robert, 67
European Union, 207
Excalibur, 86
Exposure, 29

F

Fair City, 28
Family, 40
Famine, 120, 123
Fanatic Hearts, 185
Far and Away, 15, 16
Fianna Fail party, 46, 199
Field, The, 119-124, 127, 128, 139, 189, 208
Film Base News, 159
Film Ireland, 159, 198
Fine Gael party, 46
Finnegan's Wake, 203
Finney, Albert, 134, 185
Fitzgerald, Ciaran, 181
Flaherty, Robert, 56
Fouere, Olwen, 37
Frankie Starlight, 185
Fricker, Brenda, 117, 121, 173

G

Gaeltacht, 56
Gallagher, Bronagh, 146, 147
Galway Film Fleadh, 196
Gambon, Michael, 185

M

P

Parillaud, Anne, 184
Partition, 199
Patriot Games, 127, 200
Pearson, Noel, 85, 115, 124, 133, 138, 139, 184
Pigs, 74, 119, 168, 185
Pilkington, Lorraine, 106
Playboys, The, 133-138, 149
Plunkett, Jim, 146
Poitin, 56
Postlethwaite, Pete, 126
Power in the Blood, 175, 213
Prevention of Terrorism Act, 129
Provisional IRA, 52

Q

Quiet Man, The, 7
Quinn, Bob, 56-59, 80-84, 140, 169, 185, 192, 197, 202, 207

R

Radharc, 29
Radio Telefis Eireann (RTE), 28, 34, 36, 42, 49, 51, 55, 76, 85, 106,
    152, 186, 193, 194, 203
Rea, Stephen, 86, 92
Reefer and the Model, 4, 156, 159-164, 196
Reeves, Saskia, 170
Riordans, The, 85
Road to God Knows Where, The, 180
Route 66, 174
Run of the Country, The, 133, 134, 184

S

Sayles, John, 182
Scanlan, Carol, 160
Scott, Andrew, 165
Secret of Roan Inish, The, 181-183, 213
Shaw-Smith, David, 29, 55, 202
Shellshock Rock, 174
Sheridan, Jim, 80, 85, 98, 115-133, 138, 140, 143, 197, 203, 206
Smith, Sheamus, 4, 49
Snapper, The, 39, 40, 134
Standun, Padraig, 81
Stembridge, Gerry, 185
Stoneman, Rod, 22, 189
Strongbow Films, 150, 152
Strumpet City, 28, 146
Suil Le Breith, 81
Sunrise with Sea Monster. 85

T

Thompson, Emma, 125
Tighe, Fergus, 36, 38, 71-74, 149
Toibin, Niall, 151
Tomelty, Frances, 121, 156
Toomey, Alison, 197
Traveller, 37, 38, 63, 85, 119, 156
Trevor, William, 34
Tyson, Cathy, 104

U

Ulster Television, 177

ABOUT THE AUTHOR

As a production designer, art director, and scenic artist, Terry Byrne has made a twenty-year career in New York, Dublin, and London on television, film, and live performance projects. Six of those years were spent working for Radio Telefis Eireann and for Dublin's Gate, Olympia, and Abbey theatres.

He is a graduate of the Drama Department of Carnegie-Mellon University, teaches at the College of New Jersey and is the author of *Production Design for Television.*